complete Cocktails

the perfect drink for every occasion

R&R PUBLICATIONS MARKETING PTY LTD

Published by:
R&R Publications Marketing Pty Ltd
12 Edward Street
Brunswick Victoria 3056,
Australia
Phone: (61 3) 9381 2199
Fax: (61 3) 9381 2689
Australia wide toll free 1 800 063 296
E-mail: info@randrpublications.com.au
Web: www.randrpublications.com.au
©2005 Richard Carroll

Complete Cocktails

Publisher: Richard Carroll
Mixed Drinks Research: Jon Carroll
Graphic Designer: Elain Wei Voon Loh
Project Manager: Anthony Carroll
Photography: Warren Webb, Elain Wei Voon Loh, Anthony Carroll
Stylists: Marc Phillips, Alex Reed
Proofreader: LoftCom

ISBN: 978-1-74022-566-3
First edition printed April 2005
This edition printed January 2006
Computer Typeset in Din, Piranesi
Printed in Singapore

List of sponsors as follows:
The Publishers would like to thank and acknowledge the following companies for the supply of ingredients used in the making of relevant cocktails.
- **Phillip Lazarus (Agent for Libbey Glass of America)** – Suppliers of a wide rage of glassware to the retail and hospitality trade.
- **Cadbury-Schweppes Pty. Ltd.** – Suppliers of sparkling drink mixers.
- **Carlton & United Beverages** – Suppliers of Continental Liqueurs, SKYY Vodka and many other fine spirits and liqueurs.
- **Maxxium (Aust) Pty. Ltd.** – Absolute Vodka, Galliano, Cointreau, Grant's Scotch Whisky, Glenfiddich Malt Whisky.
- **Suntory (Aust) Pty. Ltd.** – Suppliers of Midori Melon Liqueur, Rubis Strawberry Liqueur, Mohala Mango Liqueur, Lena Banana Liqueur, Frangelico, Cuervo Tequila, Tullamore Dew Irish Whiskey, Opal Nera Sambuca, Jagermeister, Chambord, Chartreuse.
- **Alpen Products Pty. Ltd.** – Suppliers of novelties, decorations and swizzle sticks.

Contents

complete Cocktails

the perfect drink for every occasion

1. Shake and strain

To shake is to mix a cocktail by shaking it in a cocktail shaker by hand. Shakers make it easy and practical to mix ingredients that do not combine easily with spirits, e.g. juices, egg whites, cream and sugar syrups.

Most shakers have two or three parts. First, fill the main part of the shaker three-quarters full with ice, then pour the ingredients on top of the ice. Less expensive ingredients should be poured before the deluxe ingredients. Shake vigorously for ten to fifteen seconds. Remove the cap or top part of the shaker and, using a Hawthorn strainer, the shaker's own built-in strainer or a knife, strain contents into the cocktail glass. This technique prevents the ice going into the glass, protecting the cocktail and ensuring melted ice won't dilute the flavor and mixture.

If you misplace the shaker cap, a coaster or the inside palm of your hand is quite effective. To sample the cocktail before serving to the customer, pour a small amount into the shaker cap and use a straw to check the taste.

2. Shake and pour

After shaking the cocktail as above, pour the contents straight into the glass, without straining out the ice. This technique is used when pouring into Hi-Ball glasses and sometimes old fashioned spirit glasses.

3. Stir and strain

To stir a cocktail is to mix the ingredients by stirring them with ice in a mixing glass and then straining them into a chilled cocktail glass. The stirring motion should be in short circular twirls. Spirits, liqueurs and vermouths that blend easily together are mixed by this method.

4. Build

To build a cocktail is to mix the ingredients in the glass in which the cocktail is to be served, pouring one on top of the other. Hi-Ball, long fruit juice and carbonated mixed cocktails are typically built using this technique. The drink should be served with a swizzle stick so that the customer can stir the ingredients. Long straws are excellent substitutes when swizzle sticks are unavailable.

5. Blend and pour

To blend a cocktail is to mix the ingredients using an electric blender or mixer. Any fruit (either fresh or tinned) should ideally be added first. Adding the fruit in small pieces gives a smoother texture than if you add the fruit whole. Next add the alcohol. Ice should always be added last. This order ensures that the fruit is blended thoroughly with the alcoholic ingredients before the ice chills the beverage.

Ideally, the blender should be on for at least 20 seconds, in order to prevent ice and fruit lumps forming that will need to be strained out. If the blender starts to rattle or hum, ice may be obstructing the blades.

Always check that the blender is clean before you start. Angostura Bitters is suitable for cleaning as it is ammonia based. Add 4 to 5 shakes to blender, fill with hot water, rinse and then wipe clean.

6. Layer or float

Layering or floating is done with ingredients that you do not want to blend with other ingredients. To do it, hold a bar spoon or dessert spoon the right way up and rest it with the lip slightly above the level of the last layer. Fill spoon gently and the contents will flow smoothly from all around the rim. Experienced bartenders use the back of the spoon.

7. Muddle

Muddling is the process of crushing or bruising fruit or mint garnishes in a glass with the muddler end of the bar spoon or with a pestle, often with some sugar and a small amount of liqueur. Other ingredients of the cocktail are added after muddling is complete. The muddling process extracts the maximum flavor from the fruit or mint. The drink can be strained after muddling if desired.

4. Sugar syrup

Sugar syrup is needed in a good cocktail bar as sugar will not dissolve easily in cold cocktails.

To make the syrup, fill a cup or bowl (depending on how much you need) with white sugar. Top up the receptacle with boiling water until just about full, and keep stirring until the sugar is fully dissolved. Refrigerate when not in use. Keeps indefinitely.

5. Sour mix

Sour mix, is also known as bar mix, is an important part of many cocktails. To make sour mix, whisk one egg white until frothy in medium-sized bowl. Mix in 1 cup of sugar, then 2 cups of water and 2 cups of lemon juice. Beat until all the sugar is dissolved. The egg whites are optional, but will make the drinks slightly foamy. Will keep in refrigerator for about a week.

6. Handling fruit juices

Never leave juices, coconut cream or other ingredients in cans. Pour them into clean bottles, cap them and refrigerate them.

Empty 25 oz/750mL glass spirit bottles make great storage bottles for fruit juices as you can attach a nip or free pourer to make it easier to pour the correct measurements. Before using the bottle, soak it in hot water to remove both the label and the flavor of the alcohol.

All the fruit cocktail recipes in this book have been tested using Berri fruit juices.

7. Handling ice

Ice is a vital ingredient of most cocktails and must be clean and fresh at all times. Small squared cubes and flat chips of ice are better for chilling and mixing cocktails. Ice cubes with holes are inefficient. Wet ice, ice scraps and broken ice should only be used in blenders.

To crush ice, fold the required amount of ice into a clean linen cloth and smash it against a solid surface. Although slightly uncivilised, this is an effective method. Don't use a bottle to hit the ice as this may shatter the bottle.

Alternatively, a blender may be used to crush ice. Half fill blender with ice and then pour in water until it reaches the level of the ice. Blend for about 30 seconds, strain out the water and you will have perfectly crushed ice. The blenders used to test these recipes were Moulinex blenders with glass jugs, which are of excellent quality. Portable ice crushers can also be purchased from some outlets.

Always use a scoop to collect the ice from an ice tray or bucket. Never pick up ice with your hands, as this is unhygienic. Shovelling a glass into an ice tray to gather ice can cause the glass to break and should be avoided.

It is important that the ice tray or bucket has been wiped clean before you put any ice into it, to ensure that the ice is kept clean.

1. Essential equipment

BARSPOON/MUDDLER OR PESTLE

BLENDER, ELECTRIC

BOTTLE OPENERS

CAN OPENER

COASTERS AND NAPKINS

COCKTAIL SHAKER

CORKSCREW AND BOTTLE OPENER OR WAITER'S FRIEND

FREE POURERS

HAND CLOTHS FOR CLEANING GLASSES

HAWTHORN STRAINER

ICE BUCKET OR TRAY

ICE SCOOP

KNIFE, CUTTING BOARD

MEASURES (JIGGERS)

MIXING GLASS

SCOOPER SPOON (LONG TEASPOON)

SWIZZLE STICKS, STRAWS

2. Glasses – helpful hints

You can serve cocktails in any type of glass, but the better, cleaner, and more sparkling the glass, the better the appearance of the cocktail. Don't use scratched, marked or colored glasses as they will spoil the appearance of the cocktail.

A good method to polish clean glasses is to hold each glass individually over a bucket of boiling water until the glass becomes steamy. Then rub the glass in a circular motion with a clean linen cloth until the glass is polished and gleaming. If the glass has a stem, hold it there while polishing to avoid marking the bowl of the glass.

All cocktail glasses should be kept chilled in a refrigerator or filled with ice while you are preparing the cocktails. An appealing effect on a glass can be achieved by running the glass under cold water and then placing it in the freezer.

All types of glasses have been designed for a specific type of drink, e.g.

- Hi-Ball glasses for long cool refreshing drinks.

- Cocktail glasses for novelty drinks.

- Champagne saucers for creamy after-dinner style drinks.

- Spirit glasses and tumblers for classic mixed drinks.

- Shot glasses for short strong drinks that are drunk in one hit (shooting).

3. Types of glasses

BEER MUG	12 oz/340mL
BRANDY BALLOON	23 oz/650mL
CHAMPAGNE FLUTE	5 oz, 7 oz/145mL, 200mL
CHAMPAGNE SAUCER	5 oz/145mL
COCKTAIL GLASS	3 oz, 5 oz, 8 oz/90mL, 145mL, 230mL
CORDIAL GLASS (EMBASSY)	1 oz/30mL
CORDIAL GLASS (LEXINGTON)	$1\frac{1}{3}$ oz/37mL
CORDIAL GLASS (TALL DUTCH)	$1\frac{1}{2}$ oz/45mL
FANCY COCKTAIL GLASS	7 oz, 10 oz/200mL, 285mL
FANCY HI-BALL GLASS	8 oz, 12 oz, 16 oz/230mL, 340mL, 460mL
FIESTA GRANDE GLASS	12 oz, 16 oz/340mL, 460mL
FOOTED PILSENER GLASS	10 oz/285mL
FOOTED HI-BALL GLASS	10 oz, 12 oz/285mL, 340mL
HI-BALL GLASS	8 oz, 10 oz, 12 oz/230mL, 285mL, 340mL
HURRICANE GLASS	8 oz, 16 oz, 23 oz/230mL, 460mL, 650mL
IRISH COFFEE GLASS	8 oz/230mL
MARGARITA GLASS	5 oz, 12 oz/145mL, 340mL
MARTINI GLASS	3 oz, 4 oz, 5 oz, 8 oz/ 90mL, 115mL, 145mL, 230mL
OLD FASHIONED SPIRIT GLASS	6 oz, 7 oz, 10 oz/170mL, 200mL, 285mL
POCO GRANDE GLASS	14 oz/400mL
PRISM ROCKS GLASS	10 oz/285mL
SALUD GRANDE GLASS	10 oz/285mL
SHOT GLASS	$1\frac{1}{2}$ oz/45mL
WINE GLASS	5 oz, 7 oz/145mL, 200mL

4. Juices, garnishes and other ingredients

ALMONDS, SLIVERED	LIMES
APPLE	MARASCHINO CHERRIES, RED
APRICOT JAM	MILK, FRESH
BANANA	MINT LEAVES
BLUEBERRIES	NUTMEG
CARBONATED WATERS	OLIVES
CELERY	ONIONS
CELERY SALT	ORANGE AND MANGO JUICE
CHOCOLATE FLAKE	ORANGES
CINNAMON	PEPPER
COCKTAIL ONIONS RED	PINEAPPLE, FRESH
COCONUT CREAM	PINEAPPLE, CRUSHED CANNED
CREAM, FRESH, SINGLE AND WHIPPED	CANTALOUPE
CUCUMBER	SALT
EGGS, FRESH	STRAWBERRIES
FLOWERS, ASSORTED PLASTIC	SUGAR AND SUGAR CUBES
FRUIT NECTAR, CANNED	SUGAR SYRUP
FRUIT PULPS, CANNED	TABASCO SAUCE
FRUIT, CANNED	TOMATOES
JELLY BABIES	VANILLA ICE CREAM
LEMON JUICE, PURE	WORCESTERSHIRE SAUCE
LEMONS	

5.
Recommended spirits

BRANDY

CAMPARI

GIN

MALIBU

OUZO

PERNOD

RUM, DARK AND LIGHT, E.G. BACARDI

SOUTHERN COMFORT

TEQUILA

VODKA, E.G. SKYY

WHISKY, E.G. GRANT'S SCOTCH WHISKY, IRISH WHISKEY, CANADIAN CLUB WHISKY, TENNESSEE WHISKEY, BOURBON

VANDERMINT

6.
Recommended Vermouth

VERMOUTH BIANCO

VERMOUTH DRY

VERMOUTH ROSSO

7. Recommended liqueurs

ADVOCAAT

AMARETTO

BAILEYS IRISH CREAM

BANANA LIQUEUR (LENA)

BENEDICTINE

CURAÇAO BLUE

CASSIS

CHARTREUSE, GREEN AND YELLOW

CHERRY ADVOCAAT

CHERRY BRANDY

CLAYTON'S TONIC (NON-ALCOHOLIC)

COCONUT LIQUEUR

COINTREAU

CRÈME DE CAFÉ

CRÈME DE MENTHE GREEN

CRÈME DE CACAO DARK

DRAMBUIE

FRANGELICO

GALLIANO

GRAND MARNIER

GRENADINE CORDIAL (NON-ALCOHOLIC)

KAHLÚA

KIRSCH

MANGO LIQUEUR (MOHALA)

MELON LIQUEUR (MIDORI)

ORANGE LIQUEUR

PEACH LIQUEUR

PIMM'S NO. 1 CUP

SAMBUCA BLACK

SAMBUCA CLEAR

STRAWBERRY LIQUEUR (RUBIS)

TIA MARIA

TRIPLE SEC (WHITE CURAÇAO)

VANDERMINT

ABSOLUT CITRON: A lemon-flavored vodka.

ABSOLUT KURANT: A blackcurrant-flavored vodka.

ADVOCAAT: A combination of fresh egg yolks, sugar, brandy, vanilla and spirit. Recommended shelf life is only 12–15 months from manufacture.

AMARETTO: A subtle liqueur with a distinct almond flavor. Amaretto (di Galliano) is a well-known brand.

AMER PICON: A bitter liqueur made with orange peel, quinine, spices and herbs. It is often used as a digestive.

AMONTILLADO SHERRY: A smooth-bodied sherry, golden-brown in color, and aged in oak casks to give it a mellow nutty flavor.

ANGOSTURA BITTERS: An essential part of any bar or kitchen. A unique flavoring whose origins date back to 1824. A secret blend of natural herbs and spices, used as a flavoring agent in both sweet and savoury dishes and drinks. Ideal for dieters as it is low in sodium and calories.

ANISETTE LIQUEUR: A liqueur flavored with anise oil.

APRICOT BRANDY: An apricot-flavored liqueur.

AQUAVIT: A Scandinavian liquor with the flavor of caraway seeds.

ARMAGNAC: A brandy made in the demarcated region of Armagnac, France.

ARRACK: A spirit distilled from the fermented sap of toddy palms or from fermented molasses.

BACARDI: A light-bodied rum. See Rum.

BAILEYS IRISH CREAM: The largest selling liqueur in the world. It is a blend of Irish whiskey, dairy cream and other flavorings. It is a natural product.

BANANA LIQUEUR (LENA): A banana-flavored liqueur.

BENEDICTINE: A brandy-based liqueur. The perfect end to a perfect meal. Serve straight, with ice, soda, or as part of a favorite cocktail.

BOURBON (WHISKEY): A type of whiskey from the USA with a smooth, easy flavor.

BRANDY: A smooth and mild spirit, mainly produced from the juice of grapes, which is considered a very smooth and palatable drink and ideal for mixing.

BUTTERSCOTCH SCHNAPPS: a butterscotch-flavored liqueur.

CALVADOS: fine apple brandy made in Normandy.

CAMPARI: A bitter Italian aperitif. Suitable both as a long or short drink, or as a key ingredient in many fashionable cocktails.

CASSIS: A rich purple liqueur that delivers the robust flavor and aroma of blackberries. Cassis lends itself to neat drinking or an endless array of delicious sauces and desserts.

CHAMBORD: A raspberry liqueur.

CHARTREUSE: A liqueur available in yellow or green. Still made by monks of the Carthusian order.

CHERI-SUISSE: A chocolate- and cherry-flavored liqueur from Switzerland.

CHERRY ADVOCAAT: A morello cherry-flavored advocaat-based liqueur.

CHERRY BRANDY: Made from concentrated morello cherry juice with a small quantity of bitter almonds and vanilla added. Enjoyable as a neat drink before or after dinner. Excellent for mixers and topping for ice cream.

CHERRY HEERING: A popular dark-red cherry-flavored liqueur made in Denmark. Known also as Peter Heering.

COCONUT LIQUEUR: A smooth liqueur with the exotic flavor of coconut heightened with light-bodied white rum.

COINTREAU: A liqueur with the aromatic orange flavor of natural citrus fruits. A great mixer and delightful over ice.

CRÈME DE BANANA: Creamy yellow liqueur very similar to banana liqueur.

CRÈME DE CACAO DARK: A rich chocolate liqueur. Smooth and classy. Serve on its own, or mix for all kinds of delectable treats.

CRÈME DE MENTHE GREEN:
A liqueur with a clear
peppermint flavor, reminiscent
of a fresh and crisp winter's
day in the mountains. An
excellent mixer.

CRÈME DE MENTHE WHITE:
As for Crème de Menthe
Green, when color is
not required.

CRÈME DE CACAO WHITE:
This liqueur delivers a
powerful and full-bodied
chocolate flavor. An excellent
mixer when a chocolate flavor
without color is desired.

CRÈME DE CAFÉ: A sweet
brown liqueur made from
extracts of coffee.

CRÈME DE CASSIS: A blood-
red, sweet, black currant-
flavored liqueur.

CRÈME DE GRAND MARNIER:
A very smooth-tasting premium
blend of Grand Marnier and
French cream, introduced to
Australia in 1985. The orange/
cognac flavor blends
beautifully with the cream.

CURAÇAO BLUE: Slightly
bitter liqueur based on
natural citrus fruits. Same
as Triple Sec but brilliant
blue color is added to make
cocktails more exciting.

CURAÇAO ORANGE: Same as Curaçao Blue, but has a strong orange color and flavor.

CURAÇAO RED: Same as Curaçao Blue, but has a strong red color.

CURAÇAO TRIPLE SEC: Also known as White Curaçao. As for Blue Curaçao, but without color. As a liqueur one of the most versatile. Can be enjoyed with or without ice as a neat drink, and is used in more mixed cocktails than any other liqueur.

DRAMBUIE: A Scotch whisky liqueur. Made from a secret recipe dating back to 1745. The names comes from 'An Dram Buidheach', meaning 'the drink that satisfies'.

DUBONNET: A wine-based aperitif from France flavored with spices and quinine.

FERNET BRANCA: A bitter, aromatic Italian spirit made from over 40 herbs and spices, with a base of grape alcohol. Often served as a digestif.

FRANGELICO: A wild-hazelnut liqueur imported from Italy. Contains infusions of berries and flowers to enrich the flavor.

GALLIANO (LIQUEUR):
A classic golden liqueur that blends with a vast array of mixed drinks. Varieties include anise, licorice and vanilla.

GIN: A grain-based spirit whose aroma comes from juniper berries and other rare and subtle herbs. The perfect mixer for both short and long drinks.

GLAYVA: A whisky-based honey and herb-flavored liqueur from Scotland, similar to Drambuie.

GRAND MARNIER: An orange-flavor liqueur, an original blend of fine old Cognac and extract of oranges. The recipe is over 150 years old.

GRAPPA: An Italian brandy made from distilling grape skins, known as a digestif.

GRENADINE CORDIAL: A grenadine-flavored non-alcoholic syrup.

IRISH WHISKEY: The distinctive national whiskey of Ireland. Irish Whiskey is distilled three times, not twice. Made from malted barley, unmalted barley, and other grains such as rye and corn.

JÄGERMEISTER: This is a bitter German aperitif flavored by a complex blend of 56 herbs, fruits and spices.

KAHLÚA: A smooth, dark Mexican liqueur made from real coffee and fine clear spirits.

KIRSCH: A fruit brandy distilled from morello cherries. Delicious drunk straight and excellent in a variety of food recipes.

MALIBU: A clear coconut liqueur based on white rum. Its distinctive taste blends naturally with virtually every mixer available.

MANDARIN NAPOLEON: A Belgian orange liqueur made from cognac flavored with oils from fresh Sicilian tangerines.

MANGO LIQUEUR (MOHALA): A mango-flavored liqueur.

MELON LIQUEUR (MIDORI): A soft green liqueur which exudes a refreshing melon flavor. Smooth on the palate. Serve on the rocks, or use to create summertime cocktails.

MINT LIQUEUR: A term for any liqueur with mint flavoring, e.g. crème de menthe, peppermint schnapps, etc.

OPAL NERA: See Sambuca Black.

ORANGE BITTERS: Bitters made from unripe orange rinds infused in alcohol. See also Angostura Bitters.

ORANGE LIQUEUR: An orange-flavored liqueur.

ORGEAT: A sweet almond-flavored syrup made also with rose water and orange-flower water.

OUZO: The traditional aperitif of Greece, but now also distilled in Australia. The distinctive flavor of this neutral grain spirit is derived mainly from the seed of the anise plant.

PARFAIT AMOUR: A light-bodied purple French liqueur made from lemons, oranges, brandy and herbs.

PASSIONFRUIT LIQUEUR (PASSOA): A passionfruit-flavored liqueur.

PEACH LIQUEUR: The delicious flavor of fresh and dried peaches make this a cocktail lover's dream.

PEACHTREE SCHNAPPS: A crystal clear spirit, bursting with the taste of ripe peaches. Drink chilled, on the rocks or mix with any soft drink or juice.

PEAR BRANDY: A digestif made from pears, sometimes sold with a pear in the bottle.

PERNOD: A anise-flavored French spirit, commonly drunk as an aperitif.

PIMM'S NO. 1 CUP: A gin-based liqueur, flavored by a secret combination of herbs and spices.

PINEAPPLE LIQUEUR: A sun-filled delight. Delicious neat, a necessity for summertime cocktails.

RUM: A spirit distilled from fermented sugar. Can be dark or light. A light-bodied rum is especially suited for cocktails in which you require subtle aroma and delicate flavor.

RYE WHISKEY (CANADIAN CLUB): Distilled from rye, corn and malted barley. A light, mild and delicate whiskey, ideal for drinking straight or in mixed cocktails.

SABRA: An Israeli liqueur with a unique flavor that comes from tangy jaffa oranges, with a hint of chocolate.

SAMBUCA BLACK: As for clear Sambuca but flavored with extracts of black elderberry. Opal Nera is a premium Sambuca. Also Galliano Sambuca Black.

SAMBUCA CLEAR: An Italian liqueur made from elderberries with a touch of anise. Also called Galliano Sambuca.

SCOTCH WHISKY (GRANT'S): The distinctive national spirit of Scotland. Made from malted barley and other grains.

SOUTHERN COMFORT: A sweet and full-bodied peach-flavored liqueur based on bourbon whiskey. Its recipe is a secret.

STRAWBERRY LIQUEUR (RUBIS): A fluorescent red liqueur with an unmistakable strawberry bouquet.

STREGA: From Italian origins, Strega is made from orange peel, spices and strong spirits. It is very sweet.

TENNESSEE WHISKEY (JACK DANIEL'S): A type of whiskey distinctive from bourbon, made from the 'old sour mash' process. It is leached through hard maple charcoal, then aged in charred white oak barrels at a controlled temperature, in order to acquire its body, bouquet and color, while remaining smooth.

TEQUILA: A spirit distilled from the sap of the agave or century plant. A perfect mixer or drink straight with salt and lemon.

TIA MARIA: A rum-based liqueur whose flavor derives from the finest Jamaican coffee. It is not too sweet with a subtle taste of coffee.

TRIPLE SEC: See Curaçao Triple Sec.

VANDERMINT: A rich chocolate liqueur with the added zest of mint.

VERMOUTH: Vermouth is a herbally infused wine, made in France and Italy. Three styles are the most prevalent: Bianco, Rosso and Dry.

VERMOUTH BIANCO:
A light, fruity and refreshing Vermouth. Mixes well with soda, 7-up and fruit juices.

VERMOUTH DRY: A crisp, light and dry Vermouth, used as a base for many cocktails.

VERMOUTH ROSSO: This Vermouth has a bitter sweet herbal flavor, and is often drunk as an aperitif.

VODKA: The second highest selling spirit in the world, generally made from grain or potatoes. Most vodkas are filtered through tanks containing charcoal to remove all odours and impurities. SKYY Vodka is a premium 40% ABV vodka that is made from the finest American grain and 100% filtered water. It is smooth-tasting and remarkably pure. Purity was the objective of SKYY's creator, American entrepreneur Maurice Kanbar, who set out to remove all of the headache-causing impurities that form during the fermentation process and to remove the fusel oils so often found in vodka-type spirits.

WEST COAST COOLER:
A white wine–based alcoholic drink with fruit flavors.

WHISKY, WHISKEY:
See bourbon whiskey, Irish whiskey, rye whiskey, Scotch whisky and Tennessee whiskey.

ABC

Ingredients

GLASS
_____
10 oz/285mL HI-BALL GLASS

MIXERS
_____
5 ICE CUBES

$^2/_3$ oz/20mL ARMAGNAC

$^2/_3$ oz/20mL
BENEDICTINE

1 dash ANGOSTURA BITTERS

CHAMPAGNE OR SPARKLING
WHITE WINE

GARNISH
_____
LEMON SLICE

ORANGE SEGMENTS

MARASCHINO CHERRIES

Method

Crack 2 ice cubes and place
them into a shaker with
Armagnac, Benedictine and
Angostura bitters and shake
well. Crush remaining ice
cubes and empty into a hi-ball
glass. Drain contents of shaker
into the crushed ice and top
with champagne. Serve
garnished with lemon slice,
orange segments and cherries.

Acapulco I

Ingredients

GLASS

10 oz/285mL HI-BALL GLASS

MIXERS

1 oz/30mL TEQUILA

1 oz/30mL DARK RUM

1 oz/30mL TIA MARIA

5 oz/145mL COCONUT CREAM

ICE CUBES

GARNISH

ORANGE SLICE

Method

Shake ingredients in a shaker.
Then strain over ice using a
Hawthorn strainer into a
10 oz/285mL hi-ball glass
and serve garnished with an
orange slice.

Affinity

Ingredients

GLASS

7 oz/200mL FANCY CHAMPAGNE GLASS

MIXERS

CRACKED ICE

2 oz/60mL GRANT'S SCOTCH WHISKY

2 dashes ANGOSTURA BITTERS

1 oz/30mL DRY VERMOUTH

1 oz/30mL SWEET VERMOUTH

GARNISH

twist LEMON PEEL

Method

Half fill a mixing glass with cracked ice, add liquid ingredients and stir. Strain into a 7 oz/200mL champagne glass, garnish with lemon peel and serve.

cocktails 𝒜

After Eight

Ingredients

GLASS

2 oz/60mL FANCY SHOOTER
GLASS

MIXERS

$^1/_2$ oz/15mL KAHLÚA

$^1/_3$ oz/10mL CRÈME DE MENTHE

$^2/_3$ oz/20mL BAILEYS IRISH
CREAM

GARNISH

twist LEMON PEEL

Method

Layer ingredients in given order
into a tall Dutch cordial glass or
fancy shooter glass and serve.

Amaretto Sour

Ingredients

GLASS

8 oz/230mL COCKTAIL GLASS

MIXERS

1 ½ oz/45mL
AMARETTO DI GALLIANO

JUICE OF ½ LEMON

SODA WATER

3 ICE CUBES

GARNISH

LIME SLICE

Method

Shake amaretto, lemon juice and ice, pour into a cocktail glass and top with soda. Garnish with a strip of lime peel and serve.

Angel's Kiss

Ingredients

GLASS

10 oz/285mL POCO GRANDE
GLASS

MIXERS

1 scoop VANILLA ICE CREAM

1 tablespoon PASSIONFRUIT PULP

5 oz/145mL APRICOT NECTAR

CRACKED ICE

GARNISH

MINT LEAVES

Method

Blend all ingredients with ice
and pour into glass. Serve
garnished with mint leaves.

Comments: A wonderful blend
of passionfruit and apricots.

Apple Strawberry Cordial

Ingredients

GLASS

7 oz/200mL OLD FASHIONED SPIRIT GLASS

MIXERS

1 APPLE, PEELED AND CORED

3 STRAWBERRIES, LEAVES REMOVED

1 oz/30mL GRANT'S SCOTCH WHISKY

1 teaspoon BROWN SUGAR

1 PINCH ALLSPICE, NUTMEG

CRACKED ICE

GARNISH

1 STRAWBERRY

GROUND NUTMEG

Method

Blend over ice and pour into glass. Garnish with a strawberry and sprinkle of nutmeg.

April Shower

Ingredients

GLASS

10 oz/285mL HI-BALL GLASS

MIXERS

1 oz/30mL BRANDY

2 oz/60mL ORANGE JUICE

1 oz/30mL BENEDICTINE

2 ICE CUBES

SODA WATER (TO TOP UP)

GARNISH

2 CHERRIES

Method

Pour all ingredients except soda into glass. Stir, top up with soda water and garnish with cherries. Serve with straws.

Aquavit Fizz

Ingredients

GLASS

6 oz/170mL TULIP CHAMPAGNE FLUTE

MIXERS

1½ oz/45mL AQUAVIT

1 oz/30mL LEMON JUICE

½ oz/15mL CHERRY HEERING

⅓ oz/10mL SUGAR SYRUP

1 EGG WHITE

SODA WATER

ICE CUBES

Method

Shake all ingredients with ice and strain into glass. Then top up with soda water.

Astronaut

Ingredients

GLASS

10 oz/285mL HI-BALL GLASS

MIXERS

1 oz/30mL DARK RUM

1 oz/30mL VODKA

$\frac{1}{3}$ oz/10mL FRESH LEMON JUICE

6 drops PASSIONFRUIT PULP

ICE CUBES

GARNISH

$\frac{1}{2}$ scoop PASSIONFRUIT

Method

Shake all ingredients over ice
and strain into glass.
Garnish with $\frac{1}{2}$ scoop
of passionfruit.

Avalanche

Ingredients

GLASS

7 oz/200mL FLUTED WINE GLASS

MIXERS

1 oz/30mL COINTREAU

1 oz/30mL ORANGE JUICE

1 oz/30mL TIA MARIA

1$\frac{2}{3}$ oz/50mL CREAM

ICE CUBES

Method

Shake all ingredients with ice.
Then strain into glass to serve.

cocktails B

B&B

Ingredients

GLASS

BRANDY BALLOON GLASS

MIXERS

1 oz/30mL COGNAC

1 oz/30mL BENEDICTINE

Method

Build, no ice.

Comments: Tempt your pallet with this delicious combination of fine liqueurs. Relaxing by the fire on winter nights, the connoisseur will enjoy interesting conversation with friends over this drink. Ideal with coffee.

B52

Ingredients

GLASS

7 oz/200mL OLD FASHIONED
SPIRIT GLASS

MIXERS

1 oz/30mL KAHLÚA

1 oz/30mL BAILEYS IRISH
CREAM

1 oz/30mL GRAND MARNIER

CRUSHED ICE

Method

Place a scoop full of crushed
ice into glass. Layer ingredients
and serve.

Bacardi Blossom

Ingredients

GLASS

3 oz/90mL FANCY MARTINI GLASS

MIXERS

1 1/3 oz/40mL BACARDI RUM

3 ICE CUBES

1/3 oz/10mL ORANGE JUICE

1/3 oz/10mL LEMON JUICE

1 teaspoon SUGAR

GARNISH

twist LEMON RIND

Method

Shake all ingredients and strain into glass. Serve garnished with lemon rind.

Bad Girl

Ingredients

GLASS

5 oz/145mL CHAMPAGNE SAUCER

MIXERS

½ oz/15mL MALIBU

⅓ oz/10mL GALLIANO LIQUEUR

½ oz/15mL BANANA LIQUEUR

1 oz/30mL CREAM

½ oz/15mL ADVOCAAT

CRACKED ICE

GARNISH

1 STRAWBERRY

Method

Blend ingredients with ice, pour into glass and serve garnished with strawberry.

Badminton

Ingredients

GLASS

8 oz/230mL RED WINE GLASS

MIXERS

5 oz/145mL RED WINE

1 teaspoon SUGAR

1 pinch NUTMEG

SODA WATER

GARNISH

CUCUMBER SLICE, CUT
LENGTHWAYS

Method

Stir sugar into red wine and
add nutmeg, then top up with
soda water. Serve garnished
with cucumber slice.

Baltimore Zoo

Ingredients

GLASS

10 oz/285mL FOOTED PILSENER GLASS

MIXERS

$^{1}/_{2}$ oz/15mL DARK RUM

$^{1}/_{2}$ oz/15mL GIN

$^{1}/_{2}$ oz/15mL COINTREAU

2 oz/60mL CRANBERRY JUICE

BEER

ICE CUBES

Method

Shake all ingredients with ice and strain into glass. Then top up with beer.

Banana Colada

Ingredients

GLASS

10 oz/285mL FANCY GLASS

MIXERS

1 oz/30mL BACARDI RUM

1 oz/30mL SUGAR SYRUP

1 oz/30mL COCONUT CREAM

1 oz/30mL CREAM

5 oz/145mL PINEAPPLE JUICE

1/2 BANANA

CRACKED ICE

GARNISH

BANANA SLICE

PINEAPPLE WEDGE AND LEAVES

SPEARMINT AND MINT LEAVES

Method

Blend with ice and pour into glass. Garnish with a slice of banana, pineapple wedge and leaves, spearmint and mint leaves. Serves with straws.

Comments: An exemplary cocktail to demonstrate the variety of fruits available, particularly in Australia. You can modify this cocktail with your own selection of exotic fruit.

Banshee

Ingredients

GLASS

BRANDY BALLOON

MIXERS

1 oz/30mL DARK RUM

2 oz/60mL CREAM

$^2/_3$ oz/20mL CRÈME DE CACAO

1 BANANA

$^1/_2$ oz/15mL BANANA LIQUEUR

GARNISH

3 CHERRIES

Method

Blend all ingredients until
smooth and pour into glass.
Serve garnished with cherries.

Bellini (Frozen)

Ingredients

GLASS

5 oz/145mL CHAMPAGNE FLUTE

MIXERS

2 oz/60mL PEACH SLICES
WITH SYRUP

1 oz/30mL VODKA

1 oz/30mL PEACH LIQUEUR

1 teaspoon SUGAR

CHAMPAGNE

CRACKED ICE

Method

Blend with ice, then strain into glass. Top up with champagne.

Belly Dancer

Ingredients

GLASS

3 oz/90mL COCKTAIL GLASS

MIXERS

1 oz/30mL CREAM

½ oz/15mL LIME JUICE

2 oz/60mL COCONUT CREAM

½ oz/15mL GRENADINE CORDIAL

ICE CUBES

GARNISH

GRATED COCONUT

Method

Shake all ingredients over ice and strain into glass. Garnish with grated coconut.

Bermuda Triangle

Ingredients

GLASS

5 oz/145mL
COCKTAIL GLASS

MIXERS

1 oz/30mL BLUE
CURAÇAO

2 oz/60mL PINEAPPLE JUICE

1 oz/30mL BACARDI RUM

CRUSHED ICE

$\frac{2}{3}$ oz/20mL AMARETTO DI
GALLIANO

GARNISH

PINEAPPLE WEDGE

Method

Blend all ingredients until
smooth, then pour into glass.
Garnish with pineapple wedge
to serve.

Betsy Ross

Ingredients

GLASS

BRANDY BALLOON

MIXERS

1 oz/30mL BRANDY

1 oz/30mL PORT WINE

1 teaspoon COINTREAU

4–5 dashes OF ANGOSTURA BITTERS

ICE CUBES

Method

Shake all ingredients over ice and strain into glass.

Between the Sheets

Ingredients

GLASS
_____

5 oz/145mL CHAMPAGNE SAUCER

MIXERS
_____

1 oz/30mL BRANDY

1 oz/30mL BACARDI RUM

1 oz/30mL COINTREAU

$\frac{1}{2}$ oz/15mL LEMON JUICE

ICE CUBES

GARNISH
_____

twist LEMON RIND

Method

Shake all ingredients with ice and strain into glass. Garnish with twist of lemon rind.

Comments: A pre-dinner cocktail. A fine blend of traditional spirits for the mature palate.

Black Velvet

Ingredients

GLASS

5 oz/145mL CHAMPAGNE SAUCER

MIXERS

2$\frac{1}{2}$ oz/70mL CHAMPAGNE

2$\frac{1}{2}$ oz/70mL STOUT

Method

Build in glass and stir.

Blackjack

Ingredients

GLASS

5 oz/145mL COCKTAIL
GLASS

MIXERS

1 oz/30mL KIRSCH

1½ oz/45mL FRESH COFFEE

⅓ oz/10mL BRANDY

CRUSHED ICE

GARNISH

COFFEE GRANULES

Method

Stir all ingredients with ice in
a mixing glass and pour into
cocktail glass. Serve garnished
with coffee granules.

Blood & Sand

Ingredients

GLASS

5 oz/145mL CHAMPAGNE SAUCER

MIXERS

1 oz/30mL GRANT'S SCOTCH WHISKY

1 oz/30mL ORANGE JUICE

1 oz/30mL CHERRY BRANDY

CRACKED ICE

1 oz/30mL SWEET VERMOUTH (ROSSO OR BIANCO)

GARNISH

1 twist ORANGE RIND

Method

Half fill mixing glass with cracked ice, add other ingredients and stir. Strain into champagne saucer and garnish with orange rind to serve.

Bloodhound

Ingredients

GLASS

5 oz/145mL COCKTAIL GLASS

MIXERS

½ oz/15mL DRY VERMOUTH

3 dashes STRAWBERRY LIQUEUR

½ oz/15mL GIN

2 STRAWBERRIES, LEAVES REMOVED

½ oz/15mL SWEET VERMOUTH (ROSSO OR BIANCO)

4 ICE CUBES

GARNISH

2 STRAWBERRIES

Method

Blend two ice cubes, gin, both types of vermouth, strawberry liqueur and two strawberries. Pour into glass over remaining ice cubes. Garnish with remaining strawberries to serve.

B cocktails

Bloody Mary

Ingredients

GLASS

10 oz/285mL HI-BALL GLASS

MIXERS

2 oz/60mL VODKA

1 dash WORCESTERSHIRE SAUCE

⅓ oz/10mL LEMON JUICE

2–3 drops TABASCO SAUCE

TOMATO JUICE

3 ICE CUBES

SALT

PEPPER

Method

Into glass pour vodka, sauces, lemon juices and a sprinkle of salt and pepper. Top up with tomato juice and ice cubes and serve with swizzle stick and straws.

Note: White rum or tequila may be used instead of vodka.

Blue French

Ingredients

GLASS

10 oz/285mL HI-BALL
GLASS

MIXERS

1 oz/30mL PERNOD

1 teaspoon LEMON
JUICE

1 teaspoon BLUE
CURAÇAO

BITTER LEMON (SOFT DRINK)

ICE CUBES

GARNISH

LEMON WHEEL

Method

Build over ice in glass. Top
up with bitter lemon. Garnish
with lemon wheel, and serve
with straws.

Blue Lagoon

Ingredients

GLASS

BRANDY BALLOON

MIXERS

1 oz/30mL GIN

1/3 oz/10mL BLUE CURAÇAO

7-UP

GARNISH

LEMON WHEEL

Method

Build gin and curaçao over ice and top up with 7-up. Garnish with lemon wheel.

Comments: Named after the movie which bears this cocktails name.

Bolshoi Punch

Ingredients

GLASS

10 oz/285mL FOOTED
HI-BALL GLASS

MIXERS

1 oz/30mL VODKA

⅓ oz/10mL DARK RUM

⅓ oz/10mL CRÈME DE CASSIS

½ oz/15mL LIME JUICE

½ oz/15mL LEMON JUICE

BITTER LEMON (SOFT DRINK)

ICE CUBES

GARNISH

1 ORANGE SLICE

1 RED CHERRY

Method

Blend all ingredients with ice
and strain into glass, then top
up with bitter lemon. Garnish
with orange slice and red cherry.

Bosom Caresser

Ingredients

GLASS

5 oz/145mL CHAMPAGNE SAUCER

MIXERS

1 oz/30mL BRANDY

½ oz/15mL ORANGE LIQUEUR

1 teaspoon GRENADINE CORDIAL

1 EGG YOLK

ICE CUBES

GARNISH

2 CHERRIES

Method

Shake all ingredients with ice and strain into glass. Garnish with two red cherries, slit on side of glass.

Comments: Close to every lady's heart! Egg yolk allows the cocktail to breathe, supporting the brandy's body and bounce. Fine on any occasion.

Boston Cream

Ingredients

GLASS

4 oz/130mL COCKTAIL GLASS

MIXERS

1 oz/30mL CREAM

$1/2$ oz/15mL LIME JUICE

1 oz/30mL COCONUT CREAM

$1/2$ oz/15mL GRENADINE CORDIAL

ICE CUBES

GARNISH

CHOCOLATE SPRINKLES

Method

Shake all ingredients over ice and strain into glass. Garnish with a cross made of chocolate sprinkles.

Bourbon Banana

Ingredients

GLASS

BRANDY BALLOON

MIXERS

1 oz/30mL BOURBON

1 oz/30mL ORANGE JUICE

1 oz/30mL KAHLÚA

1 oz/30mL CREAM

1 BANANA

CRUSHED ICE

Method

Blend ingredients with ice and serve in a brandy balloon.

Brandy Alexander

Ingredients

GLASS

5 oz/145mL CHAMPAGNE SAUCER

MIXERS

1 oz/30mL BRANDY

1 oz/30mL DARK CRÈME DE CACAO

1 teaspoon GRENADINE CORDIAL

1 oz/30mL CREAM

ICE CUBES

GARNISH

GROUND NUTMEG

1 CHERRY

Method

Shake with ice and strain. Sprinkle nutmeg over a pair of crossed plastic straws to make a cross pattern. Garnish with a cherry.

Comments: An after-dinner cocktail. An Alexander uses Green Crème de Menthe instead of Crème de Cacao. Cognac may be substituted for Brandy to deliver an exceptional aftertaste.

Brandy Crusta

Ingredients

GLASS

CHAMPAGNE SAUCER, SUGAR-FROSTED

MIXERS

3 oz/90mL BRANDY

1 dash ANGOSTURA BITTERS

3 dashes MARASCHINO

GARNISH

1 MARASCHINO CHERRY

Method

Frost rim of glass with sugar before starting. Shake all ingredients and strain into glass, being careful not to remove sugar. Garnish with cherry.

Brandy, Lime & Soda

Ingredients

GLASS

10 oz/285mL FOOTED HI-BALL GLASS

MIXERS

1 1/2 oz/45mL BRANDY

CRACKED ICE

1/2 oz/15mL LIME JUICE

SODA WATER

GARNISH

1 LIME OR LEMON WHEEL

Method

Pour brandy and lime juice over one scoop of ice into glass. Top up with soda water, garnish with lime or lemon wheel and serve with straws.

Brazilian Monk

Ingredients

GLASS

10 oz/285mL TULIP WINE GLASS

MIXERS

1 oz/30mL KAHLÚA

½ oz/15mL FRANGELICO

½ oz/15mL DARK CRÈME DE CACAO

2 scoops VANILLA ICE CREAM

CRUSHED ICE

Method

Blend all ingredients with ice and pour into glass. Garnish with a wild flower or flower petals.

Comments: Frangelico is imported from Italy and made from wild flowers infused into hazelnuts.

Brittany

Ingredients

GLASS

5 oz/145mL OLD FASHIONED
SPIRIT GLASS

MIXERS

1 oz/30mL GIN

$^1/_2$ oz/15mL AMER PICON

$^1/_3$ oz/10mL ORANGE JUICE

$^1/_3$ oz/10mL LEMON JUICE

CRUSHED ICE

Method

Blend all ingredients with
ice and pour into glass.

Bronx

Ingredients

GLASS

3 oz/90mL FANCY COCKTAIL GLASS

MIXERS

1 oz/30mL GIN

½ oz/15mL ORANGE JUICE

1 dash FRENCH VERMOUTH (WHITE)

CRACKED ICE

1 dash ITALIAN VERMOUTH (BIANCO)

GARNISH

ORANGE SLICE

Method

Shake and strain into glass. Serve garnished with orange slice.

Cabaret

Ingredients

GLASS
4 oz/130mL COCKTAIL GLASS

MIXERS
1 oz/30mL GIN

1 oz/30mL DUBONNET

1 teaspoon PERNOD

5 dashes ANGOSTURA BITTERS

ICE CUBES

GARNISH
RED CHERRY

Method

Stir in mixing glass over ice and strain into cocktail glass. Garnish with cherry.

Café De Paris

Ingredients

GLASS
4 oz/130mL COCKTAIL GLASS

MIXERS
2 oz/60mL GIN

$1/3$ oz/10mL HEAVY CREAM

1 teaspoon PERNOD

1 EGG WHITE

ICE CUBES

GARNISH
LEMON SLICE

Method

Shake all ingredients over ice and strain into glass. Garnish with slice of lemon.

Café Oscar

Ingredients

GLASS

8 oz/230mL IRISH COFFEE MUG

MIXERS

1 oz/30mL KAHLÚA

1 oz/30mL AMARETTO DI GALLIANO

HOT COFFEE

HEAVY CREAM

GARNISH

1 scoop VANILLA ICE CREAM

Method

Pour spirits into glass, then top up with coffee. Float cream on top. Garnish with ice cream.

Caper's Caper

Ingredients

GLASS

10 oz/285mL HI-BALL GLASS

MIXERS

1 oz/30mL ADVOCAAT

¼ AVOCADO

30mL FRANGELICO

1 scoop ICE CREAM

4–5 STRAWBERRIES

CRUSHED ICE

GARNISH

COFFEE BEAN

1 STRAWBERRY

Method

Blend ingredients with ice and pour into glass. Garnish with coffee bean and strawberry and serve with straws.

Cardamom Spice

Ingredients

GLASS

10 oz/285mL FOOTED HI-BALL GLASS

MIXERS

BROWN SUGAR LUMP

CARDAMOM ESSENCE

CRACKED ICE

2 oz/60mL GRANT'S SCOTCH WHISKY

Method

Infuse brown sugar lump with three drops cardamom essence. Add ice, then pour over whiskey. Stir.

Comments: The warm, sweet spicy flavor of cardamom combines with Grant's Scotch Whisky to create a sensational drink. You can also serve without the ice for a delicious winter cocktail.

Caribbean Champagne

Ingredients

GLASS

5 oz/145mL CHAMPAGNE
SAUCER

MIXERS

$3\frac{1}{2}$ oz/100mL CHAMPAGNE

1 oz/10mL BACARDI RUM

1 oz/10mL BANANA LIQUEUR

$\frac{1}{2}$ oz/15mL ORANGE BITTERS

GARNISH

BANANA SLICE

Method

Stir all ingredients without ice and pour into glass. Garnish with slice of banana.

Chablis Cup

Ingredients

GLASS

10 oz/285mL FOOTED HI-BALL GLASS

MIXERS

$^2/_3$ oz/20mL GRAND MARNIER

$^1/_2$ oz/15mL KIRSCH

1 PEACH SLICE

1 BANANA SLICE

1 ORANGE SLICE, NO RIND

1 LEMON SLICE, NO RIND

1 MINT SPRIG

2 oz/60mL CHABLIS (WINE)

GARNISH

ASSORTED FRUIT SLICES

Method

Blend all ingredients over ice, pour into glass, then top up with Chablis. Serve garnished with fruit.

Chambord Margarita

Ingredients

GLASS

12 oz/340mL MARGARITA GLASS, SALT-FROSTED

MIXERS

1$\frac{1}{2}$ oz/45mL TEQUILA

$\frac{1}{2}$ oz/15mL CHAMBORD RASPBERRY LIQUEUR

3 oz/90mL SOUR MIX

CRUSHED ICE

Method

Blend the ingredients with ice and serve.

Note: To make sour mix, see page 7.

Champagne Cocktail

Ingredients

GLASS

5 oz/145mL CHAMPAGNE FLUTE

MIXERS

1 SUGAR CUBE

6 drops ANGOSTURA BITTERS

½ oz/15mL COGNAC OR BRANDY

CHAMPAGNE OR SPARKLING
WHITE WINE

GARNISH

RED CHERRY

Method

Soak sugar cube in Angostura
Bitters in flute, before adding
brandy. Then top with
Champagne. Garnish with
red cherry (optional).

Champagne St Moritz

Ingredients

GLASS

5 oz/145mL CHAMPAGNE SAUCER

MIXERS

⅓ oz/10mL GIN

⅓ oz/10mL APRICOT BRANDY

⅓ oz/10mL ORANGE JUICE

CHAMPAGNE OR SPARKLING WHITE WINE

ICE CUBES

GARNISH

ORANGE SLICE

Method

Shake over ice and strain, then top up with Champagne. Garnish with orange slice.

Method

Shake with ice and strain into glass. Garnish with grated chocolate and cherry and coconut rind on side of glass.

Comments: Created by Leah Johns, this cocktail won first place in Seagram's National Liqueur Championships, Hobart, Tasmania, 1990.

Cherries Jubilee

Ingredients

GLASS

5 oz/145mL COCKTAIL GLASS

MIXERS

1 oz/30mL CHERRY ADVOCAAT

1 oz/30mL WHITE CRÈME DE CACAO

$\frac{1}{2}$ oz/15mL MALIBU

$1\frac{1}{2}$ oz/45mL CREAM

$\frac{1}{2}$ oz/15mL MILK

ICE CUBES

GARNISH

GRATED CHOCOLATE

1 CHERRY

COCONUT RIND

Cherry Bomb

Ingredients

GLASS

10 oz/285mL MARGARITA GLASS, SUGAR-FROSTED

MIXERS

1 teaspoon CASTER SUGAR

1 teaspoon GRENADINE CORDIAL

1 oz/30mL VODKA

½ oz/15mL CHERRY BRANDY

7-UP

CRUSHED ICE

GARNISH

ORCHID (OPTIONAL)

Method

Color sugar with grenadine and prepare glass by sugar-frosting the rim.

Blend other ingredients over ice and pour into glass, then top up with 7-up. Garnish with an orchid.

Comments: Watch as the magical color fizzes up like a Cherry Bomb.

Chi Chi

Ingredients

GLASS

CHAMPAGNE SAUCER

MIXERS

1½ oz/45mL VODKA

⅔ oz/20mL COCONUT CREAM

⅔ oz/20mL MALIBU

½ oz/15mL LIME CORDIAL

½ oz/15mL LEMON CORDIAL

1 slice PINEAPPLE

2 oz/60mL PINEAPPLE JUICE

1 dash CREAM

ICE CUBES

GARNISH

PINEAPPLE WEDGE

Method

Blend ingredients with ice until smooth. Pour into a champagne saucer and serve garnished with pineapple wedge.

Chicago

Ingredients

GLASS

5 oz/145mL COCKTAIL GLASS

MIXERS

1½ oz/45mL BRANDY

1 dash ANGOSTURA BITTERS

1 teaspoon COINTREAU

2 ICE CUBES

SPARKLING WHITE WINE

Method

Pour spirits into glass over ice, top up with white wine and serve.

Chiquita

Ingredients

GLASS

8 oz/230mL WINE GLASS

MIXERS

$1\frac{1}{2}$ oz/45mL VODKA

$\frac{1}{3}$ oz/10mL BANANA LIQUEUR

$\frac{1}{3}$ oz/10mL LIME JUICE

$\frac{1}{2}$ BANANA, SLICED

pinch SUGAR

ICE CUBES

GARNISH

BANANA SLICE

Method

Blend all ingredients with ice and pour into glass. Garnish with banana slice.

Chocolate-Covered Cherry

Ingredients

GLASS

8 oz/230mL IRISH COFFEE MUG, PREHEATED

MIXERS

1 oz/30mL CHERRY LIQUEUR

HOT CHOCOLATE

GARNISH

WHIPPING CREAM FROM AEROSOL CAN

1 RED CHERRY

Method

Pour in liqueur, then top up with hot chocolate. Garnish with whipping cream and red cherry.

Cliff Hanger

Ingredients

GLASS
_____

5 oz/145mL COCKTAIL
GLASS

MIXERS
_____

1½ oz/45mL VODKA

½ oz/15mL CHERRY HEERING

7-UP

½ oz/15mL GALLIANO LIQUEUR

Method

Place 2 ice cubes into glass,
then pour vodka and Cherry
Heering over top. Top up with
7-up, float Galliano Liqueur
and serve.

Clover Blossom

Ingredients

GLASS

10 oz/285mL HI-BALL GLASS

MIXERS

2 oz/60mL LEMON CORDIAL

1 oz/30mL LIME JUICE

1 EGG WHITE

1 dash GRENADINE CORDIAL

TONIC WATER

ICE CUBES

GARNISH

SLICE OF LEMON

MINT LEAF

Method

Blend all ingredients with ice and pour into glass. Garnish with slice of lemon, mint leaf and a straw.

Comments: A delicate fluffy concoction.

Cointreau Caipirinha

Ingredients

GLASS

6 oz/170mL PRISM ROCKS GLASS

MIXERS

1 oz/30mL COINTREAU

¼ FRESH LIME OR LEMON

CRUSHED ICE

Method

Cut lime into pieces and place in glass. Extract juice by using a pestle (muddling). Fill glass with crushed ice and add Cointreau. Stir.

Cointreauversial

Ingredients

GLASS

10 oz/285mL HI-BALL GLASS

MIXERS

$\frac{1}{3}$ oz/10mL MANGO PURÉE

2–3 STRAWBERRIES

2–3 KIWIFRUIT CHUNKS

2–3 FRESH MINT LEAVES

$\frac{2}{3}$ oz/20mL COINTREAU

$1\frac{1}{2}$ oz/45mL VODKA

$\frac{1}{3}$ oz/10mL STRAWBERRY LIQUEUR

7-UP OR SODA WATER

ICE CUBES

GARNISH

LIME WHEEL

MINT LEAF

Method

Muddle fruit and mint in a glass, build alcohol over ice, stir well. Top up with 7-up or soda water.

Columbia Skin

Ingredients

GLASS

10 oz/285mL BEER MUG

MIXERS

½ LEMON, THINLY PEELED

1 oz/30mL GRANT'S SCOTCH WHISKY

1 cup BOILING WATER

GARNISH

LEMON SLICE

Method

Pour Scotch and boiling water over lemon half. Garnish with a slice of lemon.

Commonwealth

Ingredients

GLASS

5 oz/145mL OLD FASHIONED
SPIRIT GLASS

MIXERS

1 oz/30mL CANADIAN CLUB RYE
WHISKY

½ oz/15mL VANDERMINT
LIQUEUR

½ oz/15mL LEMON JUICE

GARNISH

LEMON SLICE

Method

Shake all ingredients over ice
and strain into glass. Garnish
with a slice of lemon.

Copacabana

Ingredients

GLASS

3 oz/90mL COCKTAIL GLASS

MIXERS

1 oz/30mL APRICOT BRANDY

$^1/_2$ oz/15mL LEMON JUICE

$^1/_2$ oz/15mL BRANDY

$^1/_2$ oz/15mL COINTREAU

CRUSHED ICE

GARNISH

ORANGE WHEEL

Method

Shake all ingredients and
strain into a glass. Garnish
with orange wheel.

Copenhagen Special

Ingredients

GLASS

5 oz/145mL CHAMPAGNE FLUTE

MIXERS

1 oz/30mL AQUAVIT

1 oz/30mL ARRACK

$\frac{1}{2}$ oz/15mL LEMON JUICE

ICE CUBES

GARNISH

LEMON SLICE

Method

Shake all ingredients over ice and strain into glass. Garnish with a slice of lemon.

Crimson Tide

Ingredients

GLASS

OLD FASHIONED SPIRIT GLASS

MIXERS

6–8 FRESH RASPBERRIES

½ teaspoon SUGAR

CRUSHED ICE

⅓ oz/10mL LIME JUICE

1 oz/30mL FRANGELICO

1 oz/30mL ABSOLUT KURANT

1 dash CHAMBORD RASPBERRY LIQUEUR

GARNISH

FRESH RASPBERRIES

MINT SPRIG

Method

Muddle the raspberries and sugar in a shaker. Add ice and remaining ingredients. Shake and pour into an old fashioned glass. Garnish with fresh raspberries and a mint sprig.

Crush Bus

Ingredients

GLASS

7 oz/200mL OLD FASHIONED
SPIRIT GLASS

MIXERS

4–5 STRAWBERRIES

MINT LEAVES

$\frac{1}{2}$ oz/15mL SUGAR SYRUP

1 oz/30mL FRANGELICO

$\frac{1}{2}$ oz/15mL RUBIS STRAWBERRY
LIQUEUR

$\frac{1}{2}$ oz/15mL TIA MARIA

CRACKED ICE

Method

Muddle the strawberries, mint
and sugar in glass. Add the
remaining ingredients. Stir
vigorously and serve.

Czar's Delight

Ingredients

GLASS

10 oz/285mL OLD FASHIONED
SPIRIT GLASS

MIXERS

1 oz/30mL VODKA

2½ oz/75mL CREAM

1 oz/30mL PEPPERMINT
LIQUEUR

5 oz/145mL MILK

2 ICE CUBES

GARNISH

MINT LEAVES,
FROSTED WITH
SUGAR

Method

Shake ingredients
and pour into glass,
garnish with mint leaves
and serve.

Daiquiri (assorted)

Ingredients

GLASS

10 oz/285mL FOOTED HI-BALL
GLASS

MIXERS

1 oz/30mL LIQUEUR TO MATCH
FRUIT (MIDORI, RUBIS,
LENA OR MOHALA)

1 oz/30mL BACARDI RUM

1½ oz/45mL LEMON JUICE

½ oz/15mL LIME CORDIAL OR
SUGAR SYRUP

3–4 pieces OF APPROPRIATE
FRUIT (HONEYDEW MELON,
STRAWBERRY, BANANA OR
MANGO)

CRUSHED ICE

GARNISH

FRUIT SLICES

Method

Choose liqueur to match
desired fruit. Blend ingredients
with ice. Garnished with
appropriate fruit slices.

Daiquiri Original

Ingredients

GLASS

7 oz/200mL FANCY COCKTAIL
GLASS, CHILLED

MIXERS

3 oz/90mL WHITE RUM

1 teaspoon SUGAR

1 oz/30mL LEMON OR LIME
JUICE

ICE CUBES

GARNISH

LEMON SLICE

Method

Shake all ingredients with ice
and strain into chilled cocktail
glass. Garnish with lemon slice
and serve.

D cocktails

Daiquiri Strawberry

Ingredients

GLASS

10 oz/285mL COCKTAIL GLASS

MIXERS

3 oz/90mL WHITE RUM

1 oz/30mL LEMON JUICE

1 teaspoon STRAWBERRY LIQUEUR

2 oz/60mL MILK

10 STRAWBERRIES

CRUSHED ICE

GARNISH

1 STRAWBERRY

Method

Blend all ingredients until smooth, pour into glass, garnish with a strawberry and serve.

Death by Chocolate

Ingredients

GLASS

CHAMPAGNE SAUCER

MIXERS

1 oz/30mL BAILEYS IRISH CREAM

1 oz/30mL CRÈME DE CACAO

1 oz/30mL KAHLÚA

3 oz/90mL WHIPPING CREAM

1 oz/30mL TIA MARIA

ICE CUBES

GARNISH

GRATED CHOCOLATE

Method

Shake with ice and strain into a champagne saucer. Garnish with grated chocolate and serve.

D *cocktails*

Desert Rose

Ingredients

GLASS

10 oz/285mL FOOTED HI-BALL
GLASS

MIXERS

1 oz/30mL MIDORI MELON
LIQUEUR

2 oz/60mL PINEAPPLE JUICE

1 oz/30mL BAILEYS IRISH
CREAM

2 oz/60g CANTALOUPE

½ oz/15mL GLAYVA

CRUSHED ICE

GARNISH

PINEAPPLE WEDGE

Method

Blend all ingredients with ice
and pour into glass. Garnish
with pineapple wedge and
serve with straws.

Desert Storm

Ingredients

GLASS

5 oz/145mL FANCY COCKTAIL
GLASS

MIXERS

$\frac{1}{2}$ oz/15mL MANGO LIQUEUR

2 oz/60mL PINEAPPLE JUICE

$\frac{1}{2}$ oz/15mL BACARDI RUM

1 dash TABASCO SAUCE

$\frac{1}{2}$ oz/15mL GIN

ICE CUBES

GARNISH

2 CHERRY TOMATOES

Method

Shake with ice. Strain into
glass. Serve garnished with
cherry tomatoes.

Diplomat

Ingredients

GLASS

8 oz/230mL FOOTED HI-BALL GLASS

MIXERS

$1\frac{1}{2}$ oz/45mL VODKA

3 oz/90mL PINEAPPLE JUICE

$1\frac{1}{2}$ oz/45mL MIDORI MELON LIQUEUR

1 teaspoon LEMON JUICE

ICE CUBES

GARNISH

LIME WHEEL

Method

Shake all ingredients with ice. Strain into glass and serve with straws.

Dizzy Blond

Ingredients

GLASS

10 oz/285mL HI-BALL
GLASS

MIXERS

2 oz/60mL ADVOCAAT

1 oz/30mL PERNOD

7-UP

CRACKED ICE

GARNISH

1 MARASCHINO CHERRY

Method

Half fill glass with cracked ice
and add advocaat and Pernod.
Top up with 7-up, garnish with
cherry and serve.

Dizzy Whistle

Ingredients

GLASS

3 oz/90mL MARTINI GLASS

MIXERS

½ oz/15mL FRANGELICO

⅓ oz/10mL PINEAPPLE JUICE

⅓ oz/10mL GREEN CRÈME DE MENTHE

⅓ oz/10mL CREAM

Method

Layer pineapple juice onto Frangelico. Then shake Green Crème de Menthe with cream in shaker and layer onto cocktail.

Dolomint

Ingredients

GLASS

8 oz/230mL FANCY HI-BALL
GLASS

MIXERS

1 oz/30mL GIN

1 oz/30mL GALLIANO LIQUEUR

1 oz/30mL LIME JUICE

SODA WATER

FRESH MINT LEAVES

GARNISH

MINT SPRIG

Method

Pour alcohol and lime juice into
glass over ice and top up with
soda water. Decorate rim of
glass with sprig of mint and
add 2 fresh mint leaves.

Drambuie High

Ingredients

GLASS

10 oz/285mL FOOTED HI-BALL GLASS

MIXERS

1 oz/30mL DRAMBUIE

$^2/_3$ oz/20mL COCONUT CREAM

1 oz/30mL GOLDEN RUM

1 oz/30mL PINEAPPLE JUICE

1 oz/30mL CREAM

$^1/_2$ BANANA

1 scoop CRUSHED ICE

GARNISH

PINEAPPLE LEAVES

Method

Blend all ingredients until smooth, pour into glass. Garnish with pineapple leaves and serve.

Dubonnet Fizz

Ingredients

GLASS

10 oz/285mL HI-BALL GLASS, CHILLED

MIXERS

1 oz/30mL DUBONNET

1 oz/30mL CHERRY LIQUEUR

1 oz/30mL ORANGE JUICE

½ oz/15mL LEMON JUICE

SODA WATER

ICE CUBES

GARNISH

twist LEMON RIND

1 RED CHERRY

Method

Shake all ingredients over ice and pour into glass. Then top up with soda water. Garnish with lemon rind and red cherry.

Dyevtchka

Ingredients

GLASS

10 oz/285mL FANCY COCKTAIL
GLASS

MIXERS

1 oz/30mL VODKA

1 oz/30mL COINTREAU

²/₃ oz/20mL FRESH LIME JUICE

²/₃ oz/20mL FRESH LEMON JUICE

¹/₂ oz/15mL PINEAPPLE JUICE

ICE CUBES

GARNISH

PINEAPPLE WEDGE

CHERRIES

Method

Shake all ingredients with
ice and pour into glass.
Garnish with pineapple wedge
and cherry.

Comments: This drink will open
up the hidden secrets of the
formerly communist eastern
bloc of Europe.

Early Summer

Ingredients

GLASS

4 oz/125mL COCKTAIL GLASS

MIXERS

1 oz/30mL GIN

1 oz/30mL ORANGE JUICE

1 oz/30mL APRICOT BRANDY

1 oz/30mL CALVADOS

CRACKED ICE

GARNISH

1 slice APPLE

Method

Shake all ingredients with ice and strain into glass. Garnish with apple slice and serve.

cocktails

East Wind

Ingredients

GLASS

3 oz/90mL FANCY MARTINI
GLASS

MIXERS

1 oz/30mL VODKA

2–3 dashes WHITE RUM

$\frac{1}{2}$ oz/15mL DRY VERMOUTH

$\frac{1}{2}$ oz/15mL WHITE
VERMOUTH

CRACKED ICE

GARNISH

LIME SLICE

Method

Shake all ingredients with ice
and strain into glass to serve.

Eldorado

Ingredients

GLASS

4 oz/125mL COCKTAIL GLASS

MIXERS

1 oz/30mL WHITE RUM

1 oz/30mL ADVOCAAT

1 oz/30mL CRÈME DE CACAO

GARNISH

1 teaspoon GRATED COCONUT

Method

Shake all ingredients with ice. Strain into glass. Garnish with grated coconut to serve.

Electric Blue

Ingredients

GLASS

10 oz/285mL FOOTED HI-BALL GLASS

MIXERS

$^1/_2$ oz/15mL VODKA

1 oz/30mL DRY VERMOUTH

$^1/_2$ oz/15mL BLUE CURAÇAO

7-UP

GARNISH

LIME SLICE

Method

Pour vodka, vermouth and curaçao over ice into glass. Top up with 7-up and serve, garnished with lime slice.

Elephant Walk

Ingredients

GLASS
7 oz/200mL OLD FASHIONED
SPIRIT GLASS

MIXERS
1 oz/30mL GIN

1 dash ANGOSTURA BITTERS

1/2 oz/15mL TEQUILA

1 dash GRENADINE CORDIAL

1/2 oz/15mL ORANGE JUICE

CRACKED ICE

GARNISH
1/2 ORANGE SLICE

LEMON SLICE

1 stick CUCUMBER

Method

Fill glass with cracked ice, build
ingredients, and garnish with
fruit and cucumber. Add swizzle
stick and serve.

GARNISH

1 MARASCHINO CHERRY

Method

Half fill mixing glass with cracked ice, add ingredients and stir. Strain into glass, garnish with cherry and serve.

Emerald Queen

Ingredients

GLASS

5 oz/145mL CHAMPAGNE SAUCER

MIXERS

2 oz/60mL VODKA

⅓ oz/10mL BLUE CURAÇAO

1½ oz/45mL DRY VERMOUTH

⅔ oz/20mL GALLIANO LIQUEUR

CRACKED ICE

Eton Blazer

Ingredients

GLASS

10 oz/285mL FOOTED HI-BALL GLASS

MIXERS

1 oz/30mL GIN

$\frac{1}{2}$ oz/15mL LEMON JUICE

1 oz/30mL KIRSCH

SODA WATER

2 teaspoon SUGAR SYRUP

CRACKED ICE

GARNISH

3 MARASCHINO CHERRIES

Method

Place all ingredients except soda water and cherries into glass. Top up with soda water, garnish with cherries and serve.

Fallen Angel

Ingredients

GLASS

10 oz/285mL HI-BALL GLASS

MIXERS

1 oz/30mL ADVOCAAT

1 oz/30mL CHERRY BRANDY

7-UP

GARNISH

RED CHERRY OR STRAWBERRY

Method

Build alcohol over ice and stir. Top up with 7-up. Garnish with red cherry or strawberry. Serve with straws.

Comments: Ensure advocaat and cherry brandy is mixed thoroughly before topping up with 7-up. The unstirred version of this cocktail is known as a Ruptured Rooster.

Flirt with Dirt

Ingredients

GLASS

3 oz/90mL COCKTAIL GLASS

MIXERS

1 oz/30mL KAHLÚA
1 oz/30mL MALIBU
½ oz/15mL VANDERMINT
½ oz/15mL FRESH CREAM
ICE CUBES

GARNISH

1 MARASCHINO CHERRY

Method

Shake Kahlúa, Vandermint and Malibu with ice and strain into glass. Float cream and serve.

Fluffy Duck No. 1

Ingredients

GLASS

10 oz/285mL HI-BALL GLASS

MIXERS

1 oz/30mL BACARDI RUM

1 oz/30mL ADVOCAAT

7-UP

1 oz/30mL FRESH CREAM

GARNISH

LEMON WHEEL

Method

Build alcohol over ice. Top up with 7-up. Float cream. Garnish with a lemon wheel. Serve with straws.

Comments: Many cocktail bars shake ingredients with cream before topping up with 7-up.

Fluffy Duck No. 2

Ingredients

GLASS

5 oz/145mL CHAMPAGNE SAUCER

MIXERS

1 oz/30mL BACARDI RUM

1 oz/30mL ADVOCAAT

1 oz/30mL ORANGE JUICE

1 oz/30mL CREAM

ICE CUBES

GARNISH

1 ORANGE SLICE

1 RED CHERRY

Method

Shake all ingredients with ice and strain into glass. Garnish with orange slice and red cherry.

Comments: An after-dinner variation of the popular fluffy duck cocktail. A smoother and shorter drink.

MIXERS

$^1/_3$ oz/10mL COINTREAU

1 oz/30mL GIN

ICE CUBES

GARNISH

twist LEMON RIND

Method

Coat glass with Cointreau then pour gin into glass over ice. Garnish with lemon twist.

Flying Dutchman

Ingredients

GLASS

6 oz/170mL OLD FASHIONED SPIRIT GLASS

Fourth of July

Ingredients

GLASS

5 oz/145mL CHAMPAGNE SAUCER

MIXERS

⅔ oz/20mL BOURBON

⅔ oz/20mL KAHLÚA

⅔ oz/20mL GALLIANO LIQUEUR

⅔ oz/20mL ORANGE JUICE

⅔ oz/20mL FRESH CREAM

GARNISH

STRAWBERRY

pinch CINNAMON

Method

Shake all ingredients with ice and strain into glass. Serve sprinkled with cinnamon and garnished with strawberry.

Comments: Warm the champagne saucer with hot water, swirl the Galliano around and add the Bourbon. Shake the Kahlúa, orange juice and cream over ice. Ignite the Galliano and Bourbon and sprinkle cinnamon onto the flames to achieve a fireworks effect. Strain the shaken ingredients into glass to extinguish the flames.

A variation of this drink is the 'Flaming Love' in which the Bourbon is omitted, making the drink less alcoholic and smoother.

Frangelico Caipiroska

Ingredients

GLASS

OLD FASHIONED SPIRIT GLASS

MIXERS

8 LIME CHUNKS

1 teaspoon RAW SUGAR

1 oz/30mL FRANGELICO

1 oz/30mL VODKA

2 oz/60mL
CRANBERRY JUICE

ICE CUBES

Method

Muddle lime and sugar in glass. Add alcohol, ice and top with cranberry juice. Stir vigorously and serve.

Frangelico Luau

Ingredients

GLASS

10 oz/285mL HI-BALL GLASS

MIXERS

1½ oz/45mL FRANGELICO

7 oz/200mL PINEAPPLE JUICE

1 dash GRENADINE CORDIAL

CRACKED ICE

GARNISH

1 PINEAPPLE SLICE

PINEAPPLE LEAVES

Method

Blend all ingredients with ice
and pour into glass. Garnish
with pineapple slice and leaves.

Frangelico, Lime and Soda

GLASS

OLD FASHIONED SPIRIT GLASS

MIXERS

1 oz/30mL FRANGELICO

1/2 oz/15mL LIME CORDIAL

SODA WATER

GARNISH

LIME WEDGE

Method

Build alcohol over ice. Top up with soda water. Garnish with lime wedge to serve.

Frappé

Ingredients

GLASS

3 oz/90mL COCKTAIL GLASS

MIXERS

1 oz/30mL OF PREFERRED LIQUEUR (e.g., GREEN CRÈME DE MENTHE)

CRUSHED ICE

GARNISH

2 SHORT STRAWS

Method

Build over crushed ice. Garnish with two short straws.

Comments: Spoon the required quantity of crushed ice into the glass. You can create spectacular rainbow effects with small quantities of a range of colored liqueurs.

Green Crème de Menthe is highly recommended because it acts as a breath freshener when taken after dessert.

Freddy Fudpucker

Ingredients

GLASS

10 oz/285mL HI-BALL GLASS

MIXERS

1 oz/30mL TEQUILA

4 oz/125mL ORANGE JUICE

½ oz/15mL GALLIANO LIQUEUR

ICE CUBES

GARNISH

1 ORANGE SLICE

1 CHERRY

Method

Build tequila and orange juice over ice. Float in Galliano. Garnish with an orange slice and a cherry. Serve with straws.

$\mathcal{F}$ cocktails

French 95

Ingredients

GLASS

5 oz/145mL TULIP CHAMPAGNE
FLUTE

MIXERS

½ oz/15mL BOURBON OR
COGNAC

1 teaspoon LEMON JUICE

⅓ oz/10mL SUGAR SYRUP

CHAMPAGNE

ICE CUBES

GARNISH

SPIRAL OF LEMON RIND

Method

Shake Bourbon, lemon juice
and syrup over ice and strain
into glass. Top up with
Champagne. Garnish with
lemon spiral.

Comments: Substitute gin for
Bourbon or cognac to lower
the tempo to a French 75.

French Fantasy

Ingredients

GLASS
5 oz/145mL COCKTAIL GLASS

MIXERS
1 oz/30mL CRÈME DE GRAND MARNIER

1 oz/30mL VODKA

½ oz/15mL TIA MARIA

1 oz/30mL PINEAPPLE JUICE

1 oz/30mL ORANGE JUICE

ICE CUBES

GARNISH
BANANA SLICE

RED CHERRY

Method

Shake all ingredients with ice and strain into glass. Garnish with banana slice and red cherry.

Comments: Crème de Grand Marnier is similar to Baileys. This cocktail is really smooth and easy to drink.

Frozen Aquavit

Ingredients

GLASS

3 oz/90mL COCKTAIL GLASS

MIXERS

1 1/2 oz/45mL AQUAVIT

1/3 oz/10mL KIRSCH

1/3 oz/10mL LIME JUICE

1/3 oz/10mL SUGAR SYRUP

1/3 oz/10mL EGG WHITE

CRUSHED ICE

GARNISH

1 COCKTAIL ONION

Method

Blend all ingredients with ice and pour into glass. Garnish with cocktail onion.

Frozen Guava Daiquiri

Ingredients

GLASS

5 oz/145mL CHAMPAGNE SAUCER

MIXERS

1 oz/30mL BACARDI RUM

1 oz/30mL GUAVA NECTAR

$^1/_2$ oz/15mL LIME JUICE

$^1/_3$ oz/10mL BANANA LIQUEUR

$^1/_3$ oz/10mL SUGAR SYRUP

CRUSHED ICE

GARNISH

RED CHERRY

Method

Blend all ingredients with ice and pour into glass. Garnish with red cherry.

Frozen Mudslide

Ingredients

GLASS

10 oz/285mL POCO GRANDE GLASS

MIXERS

1 oz/30mL VODKA

$^{2}/_{3}$ oz/20mL BAILEYS IRISH CREAM

$^{2}/_{3}$ oz/20mL KAHLÚA

MILK

WHIPPED CREAM

THICKENED CHOCOLATE

ICE CUBES

GARNISH

STRAWBERRY

HUNDREDS AND THOUSANDS, CONFECTIONERY BALLS

Method

Blend alcohol with ice and pour into glass. Top up with milk then add whipped cream in a swirling motion. With a teaspoon slide in the thickened chocolate (or Ice Magic), thereby creating a Mudslide. Place strawberry on side of glass and sprinkle over hundreds and thousands.

Genoa

Ingredients

GLASS

7 oz/200mL HI-BALL GLASS

MIXERS

$^2/_3$ oz/20mL GIN

$^2/_3$ oz/20mL GRAPPA

$^1/_3$ oz/10mL SAMBUCA

$^1/_3$ oz/10mL DRY VERMOUTH

ICE CUBES

GARNISH

OLIVES

Method

Shake all ingredients over
ice and strain, then add ice.
Garnish with olives.

German Chocolate Cake

Ingredients

GLASS

10 oz/285mL HURRICANE GLASS

MIXERS

1 oz/30mL KAHLÚA

1 oz/30mL MALIBU

1 oz/30mL CHOCOLATE SYRUP

2 CHOPPED PECAN NUTS

2 scoops VANILLA ICE CREAM

CRUSHED ICE

GARNISH

CHOPPED PECANS

Method

Blend without ice and pour into glass over crushed ice. Garnish with chopped pecans.

Comments: More like a meal than a cocktail! From Germany, a country where eating and drinking are national pastimes, this delicious drink is a gastronomic after-dinner delight.

Gibson

Ingredients

GLASS

3 oz/90mL COCKTAIL GLASS

MIXERS

2 oz/60mL GIN

$\frac{1}{3}$ oz/10mL DRY VERMOUTH

GARNISH

1 COCKTAIL ONION

ICE CUBES

Method

Shake over ice and strain into glass. Garnish with one cocktail onion.

Glasgow

Ingredients

GLASS

5 oz/145mL OLD FASHIONED
SPIRIT GLASS

MIXERS

1 oz/30mL GRANT'S SCOTCH
WHISKY

⅓ oz/10mL LEMON JUICE

1 teaspoon DRY VERMOUTH

1 teaspoon ALMOND EXTRACT

ICE CUBES

GARNISH

SLIVERED RAW ALMONDS

DRIED FLOWER OR WHEAT
STALK

Method

Shake all ingredients
over ice and pour into
glass then add ice
cube. Garnish with
almonds and
a dried flower.

Goddaughter

Ingredients

GLASS

5 oz/145mL CHAMPAGNE SAUCER

MIXERS

1 oz/30mL SAMBUCA DI GALLIANO

1 oz/30mL AMARETTO DI GALLIANO

1 oz/30mL CREAM

1 teaspoon GRENADINE CORDIAL

GARNISH

CHOCOLATE FLAKES

1 STRAWBERRY

MINT LEAVES

Method

Shake all ingredients with ice and strain into glass. Garnish with chocolate flakes, strawberry and mint leaves.

Godfather

Ingredients

GLASS

7 oz/200mL OLD FASHIONED
SPIRIT GLASS

MIXERS

1 oz/30mL GRANT'S SCOTCH
WHISKY

1 oz/30mL AMARETTO DI
GALLIANO

ICE CUBES

Method

Build over ice.

Golden Cadillac

Ingredients

GLASS
3 oz/90mL COCKTAIL GLASS

MIXERS
1 oz/30mL GALLIANO LIQUEUR

1 oz/30mL WHITE CRÈME DE CACAO

1 oz/30mL FRESH CREAM

GARNISH
RED CHERRY OR STRAWBERRY

Method

Shake all ingredients with ice and strain into glass. Garnish with red cherry or strawberry.

Comments: This essence of cocoa beans will take you for the ride of your life. Cruise through this cocktail in luxurious style. Essential for all cocktail parties, anywhere, anytime!

Golden Dream

Ingredients

GLASS

5 oz/145mL COCKTAIL GLASS

MIXERS

1 oz/30mL GALLIANO LIQUEUR

⅔ oz/20mL COINTREAU

⅔ oz/20mL ORANGE JUICE

⅔ oz/20mL CREAM

ICE CUBES

GARNISH

ORANGE SLICE

1 STRAWBERRY

Method

Shake all ingredients with
ice and strain into glass.
Garnish with orange slice and
a strawberry on a toothpick
on side of glass.

Golden Slipper

Ingredients

GLASS

3 oz/90mL COCKTAIL GLASS

MIXERS

1 oz/30mL YELLOW
CHARTREUSE

⅓ oz/10mL APRICOT BRANDY

1 EGG YOLK

Method

Shake over ice and strain
into glass.

Grasshopper

Ingredients

GLASS

5 oz/145mL CHAMPAGNE SAUCER

MIXERS

1 oz/30mL GREEN CRÈME DE MENTHE

1 oz/30mL WHITE CRÈME DE CACAO

1 oz/30mL CREAM

CRUSHED ICE

GARNISH

2 RED CHERRIES

Method

Shake all ingredients with ice until smooth and strain into glass. Garnish with two red cherries slit on the side of the glass.

Comments: Jump right into this very popular after-dinner cocktail. Some people prefer Dark Crème de Cacao instead of White Crème de Cacao.

Variations: Add Vodka to create a Flying Grasshopper.

Greenback

Ingredients

GLASS

3 oz/90mL COCKTAIL GLASS

MIXERS

1 oz/30mL GIN

⅓ oz/10mL LIME JUICE

⅓ oz/10mL GREEN CRÈME DE MENTHE

CRACKED ICE

GARNISH

1 LIME SLICE (OPTIONAL)

Method

Stir all ingredients over ice in mixing glass and pour into glass. Garnish with lime slice (optional).

Hair of The Dog

Ingredients

GLASS

8 oz/230mL OLD FASHIONED
SPIRIT GLASS

MIXERS

2 oz/60mL GRANT'S SCOTCH
WHISKY

1 oz/30mL HONEY

2 oz/60mL CREAM

ICE CUBES

Method

Fill glass with ice, shake other
ingredients and strain over ice
into glass. Serve garnished
with flower.

Harvey Wallbanger

Ingredients

GLASS

10 oz/285mL HI-BALL GLASS

MIXERS

1½ oz/45mL VODKA

4 oz/125mL ORANGE JUICE

½ oz/15mL GALLIANO LIQUEUR

ICE CUBES

GARNISH

1 ORANGE SLICE

1 CHERRY

Method

Build vodka and orange juice over ice. Float in Galliano. Garnish with orange slice and cherry. Serve with swizzle stick and straws.

Comments: Hawaiian bartenders will tell you a visiting Irishman called Harvey ricocheted down the corridor to his hotel room after a night out. After that he was known as 'Harvey Wallbanger'.

Hawaiian Punch

Ingredients

GLASS

9 oz/270mL FANCY COCKTAIL GLASS

MIXERS

$^2/_3$ oz/20mL SOUTHERN COMFORT

$^2/_3$ oz/20mL AMARETTO DI GALLIANO

$^1/_2$ oz/15mL VODKA

$1^1/_2$ oz/45mL PINEAPPLE JUICE

$1^1/_2$ oz/45mL ORANGE JUICE

$^2/_3$ oz/20mL LIME JUICE

$^2/_3$ oz/20mL GRENADINE CORDIAL

ICE CUBES

GARNISH

THIN WEDGE OF LIME SQUEEZE

THIN WEDGE OF LEMON SQUEEZE

SLICE OF ORANGE

Method

Shake all ingredients except Grenadine over ice and pour. Add Grenadine. Garnish with squeeze of lime juice and lemon juice and slice of orange.

Heartbreaker

Ingredients

GLASS
8 oz/230mL COLADA GLASS

MIXERS
1 oz/30mL STRAWBERRY LIQUEUR

2 oz/60mL CREAM

$\frac{1}{2}$ oz/15mL TIA MARIA

4 STRAWBERRIES

$\frac{1}{2}$ oz/15mL COINTREAU

CRUSHED ICE

GARNISH
STRAWBERRY

Method
Blend until smooth and pour into glass. Serve garnished with strawberry.

Hellraiser

Ingredients

GLASS

FANCY SHOT GLASS

MIXERS

$1/3$ oz/10mL RUBIS STRAWBERRY
LIQUEUR

$1/3$ oz/10mL MIDORI MELON
LIQUEUR

$1/3$ oz/10mL OPAL NERA
(SAMBUCA)

Method

Layer in order.

Comments: Shoot this one
down – its a hell of a drink!

Hemingway

Ingredients

GLASS

5 oz/145mL CHAMPAGNE SAUCER

MIXERS

1½ oz/45mL COINTREAU

1½ oz/45mL GRAPEFRUIT JUICE

1½ oz/45mL BACARDI RUM

CRACKED ICE

SPARKLING WHITE WINE

Method

Shake all ingredients with ice except sparkling wine. Strain into a 5 oz/145mL champagne saucer. Top up with white wine and serve.

Hollywood Nights

Ingredients

GLASS

10 oz/285mL HI-BALL GLASS

MIXERS

1 oz/30mL VODKA

$^1/_2$ oz/15mL PEACH LIQUEUR

$^1/_3$ oz/10mL MIDORI MELON LIQUEUR

1 oz/30mL PINEAPPLE JUICE

SODA WATER

CRACKED ICE

Method

Three-quarters fill glass with ice, add vodka, peach liqueur and pineapple juice. Add soda water until $^1/_2$ in/1cm from top. Float Midori, add straws and serve.

Honey Bee

Ingredients

GLASS

5 oz/145mL COCKTAIL GLASS

MIXERS

1 oz/30mL BRANDY

$^1/_2$ oz/15mL HONEY

$^1/_2$ oz/15mL GALLIANO LIQUEUR

2 oz/60mL CREAM

$^1/_2$ oz/15mL GRENADINE CORDIAL

CRACKED ICE

Method

Shake all ingredients vigorously and strain into glass. Serve garnished with flower.

Honey Flow

Ingredients

GLASS

5 oz/145mL CHAMPAGNE SAUCER

MIXERS

1 oz/30mL BACARDI RUM

1½ oz/45mL CREAM

½ oz/15mL GALLIANO LIQUEUR

½ oz/15mL HONEY

CRACKED ICE

GARNISH

1 MARASCHINO CHERRY

Method

Shake all ingredients and strain into glass. Garnish with cherry and serve.

Horse Guards

Ingredients

GLASS
10 oz/285mL TUMBLER GLASS

MIXERS
2/3 oz/20mL DARK RUM

1 EGG YOLK

2/3 oz/20mL COINTREAU

SPARKLING WHITE WINE

3 ICE CUBES

GARNISH
1 SPIRAL LEMON RIND

Method

Shake ingredients except wine. Strain into glass, top up with wine and garnish with lemon rind and serve.

Hot Buttered Rum

Ingredients

GLASS

8 oz/230mL IRISH COFFEE MUG, PREHEATED

MIXERS

2 oz/60mL DARK RUM

1 LEMON SLICE

1 CINNAMON STICK

1 CLOVE

APPLE CIDER, WARMED

GARNISH

$\frac{1}{3}$ oz/10mL UNSALTED BUTTER

NUTMEG

Method

Build rum over lemon and spices and top up with warm apple cider. Garnish with butter and nutmeg.

Hot Whiskey Toddy

Ingredients

GLASS
8 oz/230mL TUMBLER

MIXERS
1 oz/30mL TULLAMORE DEW IRISH WHISKEY

SUGAR TO TASTE

BOILING WATER

GARNISH
LEMON SLICE

CLOVES

GROUND NUTMEG

Method

Build whiskey over lemon slice studded with cloves and sugar. Top up with boiling water then stir. Garnish with nutmeg. You should pour the whiskey over the lemon slice to bring out the flavor.

Hurricane

Ingredients

GLASS

12 oz/340mL HURRICANE GLASS

MIXERS

1 oz/30mL BACARDI RUM

1 oz/30mL PASSIONFRUIT LIQUEUR

$^1/_2$ oz/15mL LEMON CORDIAL

$1^1/_2$ oz/45mL LEMON JUICE

$1^1/_2$ oz/45mL SUGAR SYRUP

$^1/_2$ oz/15mL BACARDI GOLD RUM

CRUSHED ICE

GARNISH

ORANGE SLICE

Method

Shake all ingredients except Bacardi with ice and pour into glass. Float in Bacardi Gold and garnish with orange slice.

g cocktails

Ice Kacang

Ingredients

GLASS

12 oz/340mL TUMBLER GLASS

MIXERS

1 oz/30mL VODKA

½ oz/15mL PEACH LIQUEUR

1 oz/30mL CRANBERRY JUICE

1 oz/30mL ORANGE JUICE

7-UP

DICED FRUIT PIECES

CRUSHED OR SHAVED ICE

Method

Stir ingredients in mixing glass and pour over crushed ice into cooler glass. Serve with two straws and a long spoon.

Comments: Ice or es kacang is known as a dessert from the old Portuguese trading port of Malacca, East Malaysia. This cocktail variation is perfect for hot summer nights.

Independence

Ingredients

GLASS
4 oz/125mL FANCY COCKTAIL GLASS

MIXERS
1 oz/30 mL
BOURBON
¹/₂ oz/15mL LEMON JUICE
¹/₂ oz/15mL BRANDY
2 oz/60mL ORANGE JUICE
ICE CUBES

GARNISH
1 MINT SPRIG

Method
Shake all ingredients with ice and strain into glass. Garnish with sprig of mint and serve.

Inspiration

Ingredients

GLASS

5 oz/145mL COCKTAIL GLASS

MIXERS

1½ oz/45mL FRANGELICO

2 oz/60mL PINEAPPLE JUICE

½ oz/15mL BANANA LIQUEUR

1 oz/30mL CREAM

ICE CUBES

GARNISH

STRAWBERRY

MINT LEAF

Method

Shake all ingredients with ice and strain into glass. Garnish with a strawberry and mint leaf on rim and serve.

Intimate

Ingredients

GLASS

3 oz/90mL COCKTAIL GLASS

MIXERS

$^2/_3$ oz/20mL VODKA

$^2/_3$ oz/20mL APRICOT BRANDY

$^2/_3$ oz/20mL DRY VERMOUTH

ICE CUBES

2 dashes ORANGE BITTERS

GARNISH

1 BLACK OLIVE

1 twist LEMON RIND

Method

Stir all ingredients in mixing glass and strain into cocktail glass. Garnish with olive and lemon rind and serve.

Irish Coffee (Baileys)

Ingredients

GLASS

8 oz/230mL IRISH COFFEE GLASS

MIXERS

1 oz/30mL BAILEYS IRISH CREAM

1 teaspoon BROWN SUGAR

HOT BLACK COFFEE

1 oz/30mL FRESH WHIPPED CREAM

GARNISH

CHOCOLATE FLAKES OR CHOCOLATE POWDER (OPTIONAL)

Method

Stir sugar into Baileys. Top up with coffee. Float fresh cream.

Comments: Baileys Irish Coffee is one of the most popular liqueur coffees. To make Irish coffee with whiskey, substitute a good Irish whiskey such as Tullamore Dew or Jameson's for the Baileys in the recipe above. Other liqueur coffees are: French – Brandy, English – Gin, Russian – Vodka, American – Bourbon, Calypso – Dark Rum, Jamaican – Tia Maria, Parisienne – Grand Marnier, Mexican – Kahlúa, Monks – Benedictine, Scottish – Scotch, Canadian – Rye.

Iron Lady

Ingredients

GLASS

4 oz/125mL MARGARITA GLASS

MIXERS

$^1/_2$ oz/15mL MALIBU

1$^1/_2$ oz/45mL CREAM

$^2/_3$ oz/20mL RUBIS STRAWBERRY LIQUEUR

1 teaspoon VANILLA EXTRACT

$^1/_2$ oz/15mL WHITE CRÈME DE CACAO

1 Scoop VANILLA ICE CREAM

Method

Blend all ingredients until smooth, pour into glass and serve.

Island Cooler

Ingredients

GLASS

5 oz/145mL CHAMPAGNE SAUCER

MIXERS

½ oz/15mL VODKA

1 oz/30mL ORANGE JUICE

2 scoops CRUSHED ICE

2 drops GRENADINE CORDIAL

1 oz/30mL MIDORI MELON LIQUEUR

¼ KIWIFRUIT

⅓ oz/10mL LEMON JUICE

GARNISH

KIWIFRUIT SLICE

Method

Blend vodka, orange juice and ice until it is a frozen slurry. Pour into champagne saucer then add Grenadine. Blend Midori, kiwifruit and lemon juice and add to glass. Serve garnished with slice of kiwifruit.

Italian Streaker

Ingredients

GLASS

4 oz/125mL COCKTAIL GLASS

MIXERS

1 1/2 oz/45mL CREAM

1/2 oz/15mL GALLIANO LIQUEUR

1 oz/30mL ANISETTE LIQUEUR

ICE CUBES

GARNISH

ORANGE SLICE

Method

Shake over ice and pour.
Garnish with an orange slice.

Variations: Pernod may be used
as a substitute for anisette.

Jelly Bean

Ingredients

GLASS

10 oz/285mL HI-BALL GLASS

MIXERS

1 oz/30mL OUZO

½ oz/15mL BLUE CURAÇAO

½ oz/15mL GRENADINE CORDIAL

7-UP

ICE CUBES

GARNISH

1 RED CHERRY

Method

Build all ingredients except 7-up in glass over ice. Top up with 7-up. Garnish with a swizzle stick and straws and cherry dropped into glass.

Comments: A cool liquid confectionery. Dropping the Blue Curaçao and Grenadine into the cocktail after presenting to the customer, instead of building, gives a swirling lollipop effect. Regularly made without the Blue Curaçao.

Joburg

Ingredients

GLASS

5 oz/145mL OLD FASHIONED SPIRIT GLASS

MIXERS

1 oz/30mL BACARDI RUM

1/2 oz/15mL DUBONNET

3 dashes ORANGE BITTERS

ICE CUBES

GARNISH

1 twist ORANGE RIND

Method

Shake over ice and strain into glass, then add fresh ice cubes. Garnish with a twist of orange rind.

KGB

Ingredients

GLASS

6 oz/170mL OLD FASHIONED SPIRIT GLASS

MIXERS

1 oz/30mL KAHLÚA

1 oz/30mL GRAND MARNIER

1 oz/30mL BAILEYS IRISH CREAM

ICE CUBES

Method

Build over ice.

Comments: The first letter of each of the ingredients give this cocktail its name. A late night party drink.

Kakuri

Ingredients

GLASS

3 oz/90mL COCKTAIL GLASS

MIXERS

1 oz/30mL PIMM'S NO. 1 CUP

1 teaspoon LEMON JUICE

1/2 oz/15mL MANGO LIQUEUR

ICE CUBES

1/2 oz/15mL BIANCO VERMOUTH

Method

Shake all ingredients and strain into glass. Serve with swizzle stick.

Keep Going

Ingredients

GLASS

10 oz/285mL FOOTED HI-BALL GLASS

MIXERS

1 oz/30mL WHITE RUM

$\frac{1}{2}$ oz/15mL GRAPEFRUIT JUICE

$\frac{1}{2}$ oz/15mL PERNOD

1 oz/30mL COLA TONIC

$\frac{1}{2}$ slice LEMON

$\frac{1}{2}$ oz/15mL LIME JUICE

CRACKED ICE

7-UP

GARNISH

1 slice OF LEMON

Method

Half fill glass with cracked ice, shake ingredients and strain into glass. Serve garnished with slice of lemon and straws.

Kelly's Comfort

Ingredients

GLASS

10 oz/285mL FOOTED HI-BALL GLASS

MIXERS

1 oz/30mL SOUTHERN COMFORT

$^1/_2$ oz/15mL SUGAR SYRUP

1 oz/30mL BAILEYS IRISH CREAM

3 STRAWBERRIES

2 oz/60mL MILK

CRUSHED ICE

GARNISH

1 STRAWBERRY

Method

Blend all ingredients until smooth and pour into glass. Serve garnished with strawberry and straws.

Kick in the Balls

Ingredients

GLASS

5 oz/145mL CHAMPAGNE SAUCER

MIXERS

1 oz/30mL DARK RUM

1 oz/30mL ORANGE JUICE

1 oz/30mL MIDORI MELON LIQUEUR

1 oz/30mL CREAM

1/2 oz/15mL COCONUT CREAM

ICE CUBES

GARNISH

2 MELON BALLS, MARINATED IN THE RUM ABOVE

Method

Shake all ingredients with ice and strain into glass. Garnish with two marinated melon balls.

Comments: Use a toothpick to eat both balls together and you'll be sure to feel a 'Kick in the Balls'. Refrigerate melon balls when marinating to preserve their freshness.

KIR

Ingredients

GLASS

5 oz/145mL WINE GLASS

MIXERS

½ oz/15mL CASSIS LIQUEUR

DRY WHITE WINE

Method

Pour cassis liqueur into glass. then top up with dry white wine. No ice.

Comments: A superb pre-dinner drink. Use cold dry wines. Do not spoil the drink by using more than ½ oz/15mL of Cassis liqueur.

Variations: To make a Kir Imperial substitute 1 teaspoon Grenadine for ½ oz/15mL Cassis. Said to have been named after a former mayor of Dijon, France. Kir Royale is served in a 5 oz/145mL champagne flute with of 1 teaspoon Cassis liqueur topped with the best champagne available. Always remember, the better the champagne, the better the drink.

Hint: With Kir Royale sprinkle a thumb pinch of sugar into glass to produce fizzy bubbles from the white wine. Served chilled.

Klondyke

Ingredients

GLASS

3 oz/90mL COCKTAIL GLASS

MIXERS

1½ oz/45mL CALVADOS

½ oz/15mL DRY VERMOUTH

1 dash ANGOSTURA BITTERS

ICE CUBES

GARNISH

1 OLIVE

1 strip LEMON RIND

Method

Mix ingredients in mixing glass and strain into glass. Serve garnished with olive and lemon rind.

Knockout

Ingredients

GLASS

10 oz/285mL FOOTED PILSENER
GLASS

MIXERS

1 oz/30mL GRANT'S SCOTCH
WHISKY

1 EGG YOLK

$1/3$ oz/10mL SUGAR SYRUP

CRACKED ICE

SPARKLING WHITE WINE

GARNISH

1 strip ORANGE RIND

Method

Shake all ingredients except
wine and strain into glass.
Top up with wine and serve
garnished with orange rind.

L cocktails

Lady in Red

Ingredients

GLASS

5 oz/145mL CHAMPAGNE
SAUCER

MIXERS

1 oz/30mL VODKA

1/3 oz/10mL LEMON JUICE

1 oz/30mL STRAWBERRY
LIQUEUR

1 dash EGG WHITE

1/3 oz/10mL
GRENADINE
CORDIAL

4 STRAWBERRIES

1 CRACKED ICE

GARNISH

STRAWBERRY

Method

Blend with ice and pour into
a champagne saucer. Serve
garnished with strawberry.

Lady Love

Ingredients

GLASS

5 oz/145mL FANCY COCKTAIL
GLASS

MIXERS

1 oz/30mL VODKA

1 oz/30mL GALLIANO LIQUEUR

1 oz/30mL DRY VERMOUTH

1 oz/30mL ORANGE CURAÇAO

CRACKED ICE

GARNISH

1 twist ORANGE RIND

Method

Shake all ingredients and strain
into glass. Garnish with orange
rind to serve.

Lady Lynne

Ingredients

GLASS

5 oz/145mL CHAMPAGNE SAUCER

MIXERS

1¹⁄₂ oz/45mL GIN

¹⁄₃ oz/10mL LIME JUICE

1 oz/30mL PARFAIT AMOUR

ICE CUBES

1 dash EGG WHITE

GARNISH

1 STRAWBERRY

Method

Shake all ingredients
with ice and strain
into champagne saucer.
Garnish with strawberry
and serve.

Last Emperor

Ingredients

GLASS

5 oz/145mL FOOTED COCKTAIL GLASS

MIXERS

1 oz/30mL CANADIAN CLUB RYE WHISKY

1 oz/30mL BIANCO VERMOUTH

½ oz/15mL GRAND MARNIER

1 oz/30mL ORANGE JUICE

1 dash ANGOSTURA BITTERS

CRACKED ICE

GARNISH

1 strip ORANGE RIND

Method

Pour all ingredients into glass over ice. Add strip of orange rind and serve.

Lena

Ingredients

GLASS

5 oz/145mL COCKTAIL GLASS

MIXERS

2 oz/60mL BOURBON

$^1/_2$ oz/15mL CAMPARI

1 oz/30mL ROSSO VERMOUTH

$^1/_2$ oz/15mL GALLIANO LIQUEUR

$^1/_2$ oz/15mL DRY VERMOUTH

ICE CUBES

GARNISH

1 MARASCHINO CHERRY

Method

Stir all ingredients over ice in mixing glass and strain into glass. Garnish with cherry and serve.

cocktails **L**

Leprechaun

Ingredients

GARNISH

LIME SLICE

Method

Build over ice. Garnish with a lime slice dropped into the glass.

GLASS

8 oz/230mL OLD FASHIONED SPIRITED GLASS

MIXERS

2 oz/60mL TULLAMORE DEW IRISH WHISKEY

6 oz/170mL TONIC WATER

Lights of Havana

Ingredients

GLASS

10 oz/285mL HI-BALL GLASS

MIXERS

1½ oz/45mL MALIBU

1 oz/30mL MIDORI MELON LIQUEUR

2 oz/60mL ORANGE JUICE

2 oz/60mL PINEAPPLE JUICE

ICE CUBES

GARNISH

2 oz/60mL SODA WATER

LIME WHEEL

Method

Shake all ingredients over ice and pour into glass. Garnish with a straw and a lime wheel.

London Fog

Ingredients

GLASS

3 oz/90mL COCKTAIL GLASS

MIXERS

⅓ oz/10mL WHITE CRÈME DE MENTHE

1 teaspoon ANISETTE LIQUEUR

2 dashes ANGOSTURA BITTERS

ICE CUBES

GARNISH

MINT SPRIG

Method

Stir in mixing glass with over ice and strain into cocktail glass. Garnish with a mint sprig.

Comments: Anisette liqueur is a French brand of liquorice-flavored liqueur made from anise seed. Pernod may be substituted.

Long Island Iced Tea

Ingredients

GLASS

10 oz/285mL HI-BALL GLASS

MIXERS

1 oz/30mL TEQUILA

1 oz/30mL GIN

1 oz/30mL VODKA

1 oz/30mL BACARDI RUM

1 oz/30mL COINTREAU

1 oz/30mL LEMON JUICE

$^1/_2$ oz/15mL COLA (TO COLOR ONLY)

ICE CUBES

GARNISH

1 twist LEMON RIND

MINT LEAVES

Method

Build in the glass and stir. Garnish with a lemon twist and mint leaves.

Long Neck

Ingredients

GLASS

10 oz/285mL OLD FASHIONED
SPIRIT GLASS

MIXERS

1$\frac{1}{2}$ oz/45mL VODKA

1 oz/30mL MIDORI MELON
LIQUEUR

1 scoop CRUSHED ICE

1 oz/30mL LEMON JUICE

1 dash GRENADINE
CORDIAL

Method

Blend all ingredients
except Grenadine until
frozen, place in glass.
Add Grenadine and serve.

Love Potion Number 9

Ingredients

GLASS

5 oz/145mL CHAMPAGNE SAUCER

MIXERS

$2^{1}/_{2}$ oz/60mL BACARDI RUM

$^{1}/_{2}$ EGG WHITE

1 oz/30mL COINTREAU

CRACKED ICE

$^{1}/_{2}$ oz/15mL LEMON JUICE

GARNISH

1 MARASCHINO CHERRY
(OPTIONAL)

Method

Shake all ingredients and strain into champagne saucer. Garnish with cherry and serve.

Lover

Ingredients

GLASS

5 oz/145mL FANCY COCKTAIL GLASS

MIXERS

2 oz/60mL GRANT'S SCOTCH WHISKY

1 oz/30mL CAMPARI

1 oz/30mL BIANCO VERMOUTH

CRACKED ICE

GARNISH

1 twist ORANGE RIND

Method

Shake all ingredients and strain into a fancy cocktail glass. Garnish with orange rind and serve.

Lucky Dip

Ingredients

GLASS

5 oz/145mL FANCY COCKTAIL
GLASS

MIXERS

2 oz/60mL VODKA

½ EGG WHITE

1 oz/30mL CRÈME DE BANANA

1 oz/30mL LEMON SQUASH

CRACKED ICE

GARNISH

LEMON WHEEL

Method

Shake all ingredients and
strain into a fancy cocktail
glass. Serve garnished
with wheel of lemon.

Lynchburg Lemonade

Ingredients

GLASS

10 oz/285mL HI-BALL GLASS

MIXERS

⅔ oz/20mL JACK DANIEL'S TENNESSE WHISKEY

⅔ oz/20mL COINTREAU

⅔ oz/20mL FRESH LIME JUICE

7-UP OR SODA WATER

GARNISH

1 strip LEMON PEEL

Method

Pour in order then top up with 7-up or soda water. Serve garnished with twisted lemon rind.

Comments: This delicious cocktail originates from the home of Jack Daniel's.

Machine Gun Kelly

Ingredients

GLASS

5 oz/145mL CHAMPAGNE SAUCER

MIXERS

1½ oz/45mL GRANT'S SCOTCH WHISKY

1 dash ORANGE BITTERS

1 oz/30mL SWEET VERMOUTH

1 oz/30mL DRY VERMOUTH

CRACKED ICE

GARNISH

1 twist LEMON RIND

Method

Shake all ingredients and strain into champagne saucer. Garnish with lemon rind and serve.

Madame Butterfly

Ingredients

GLASS

7 oz/200mL MARGARITA GLASS

MIXERS 1

1 oz/30mL PASSIONFRUIT
LIQUEUR (OR ½ PASSIONFRUIT)

½ oz/15mL MIDORI
MELON LIQUEUR

½ oz/15mL WHITE
CRÈME DE CACAO

1 oz/30mL PINEAPPLE JUICE

CRACKED ICE

MIXERS 2

1 oz/30mL CREAM

½ oz/15mL MIDORI MELON
LIQUEUR

GARNISH

1 STRAWBERRY

BUTTERFLY ORNAMENT

Method

Shake passionfruit liqueur,
Midori, Crème de Cacao and
pineapple juice with ice and
strain into glass. Shake Midori
and cream, then float into
glass. Garnish with strawberry
and butterfly ornament.

Madras

Ingredients

GLASS

6 oz/170mL TULIP CHAMPAGNE FLUTE

MIXERS

1 oz/30mL VODKA

3 oz/90mL CRANBERRY JUICE

1 oz/30mL ORANGE JUICE

CRUSHED ICE

Method

Build vodka and cranberry juice over ice float in orange juice to top up.

cocktails M

Malibu Magic

Ingredients

GLASS

10 oz/285mL FOOTED HI-BALL GLASS

MIXERS

1 oz/30mL MALIBU

5 STRAWBERRIES

1 oz/30mL STRAWBERRY LIQUEUR

2 oz/60mL CREAM

1 oz/30mL ORANGE JUICE

CRACKED ICE

GARNISH

1 STRAWBERRY

Method

Blend all ingredients and pour into glass. Garnish with strawberry and straws, and serve.

Mama Rosa

Ingredients

GLASS

10 oz/285mL FOOTED PILSENER GLASS

MIXERS

1 oz/30mL SAMBUCA

1 oz/30mL CHERRY ADVOCAAT

SODA WATER

ICE CUBES

GARNISH

MARASCHINO CHERRY

PINEAPPLE LEAVES

ORANGE SLICE

Method

Build Sambuca and Advocaat over ice then top up with soda water. Garnish with maraschino cherry, pineapple leaves and orange slice.

Mandarin Sling

Ingredients

GLASS

5 oz/145mL
CHAMPAGNE
SAUCER

MIXERS

²/₃ oz/20mL KAHLÚA

²/₃ oz/20mL DARK CRÈME DE CACAO

¹/₃ oz/10mL CHOCOLATE SYRUP

2 scoops ORANGE SHERBET

¹/₂ MANDARIN

GARNISH

SLICE OF MANDARIN OR ORANGE

Method

Blend all ingredients without ice. Garnish with a mandarin or orange slice.

Comments: At the Mandarin Hotel in Orchard Road, Singapore, this citrus-based cocktail is a favorite.

M *cocktails*

Manhattan

Ingredients

GLASS

3 oz/90mL COCKTAIL GLASS

MIXERS

1 oz/30mL BOURBON

½ oz/15mL ROSSO VERMOUTH

dash ANGOSTURA BITTERS

GARNISH

RED CHERRY

Method

Stir all ingredients over ice and strain into glass. Garnish with a red cherry on toothpick in glass.

Comments: A pre-dinner cocktail. Frequently served to overseas guests, particularly New Yorkers.

Variations: Replace Rosso Vermouth with Cinzano Dry, add a twist of lemon and you have instantly mixed a Dry Manhattan.

Rye Whiskey may be substituted for Bourbon.

Margarita (assorted)

Ingredients

GLASS

12 oz/340mL MARGARITA GLASS, SALT-FROSTED

MIXERS

1 oz/30mL LIQUEUR TO MATCH FRUIT AVAILABLE (MIDORI, RUBIS, LENA, MOHALA)

1 oz/30mL TEQUILA

1½ oz/45mL LEMON JUICE

½ oz/15mL LIME CORDIAL OR SUGAR SYRUP

2–3 pieces OF FRUIT TO MATCH LIQUEUR (HONEYDEW MELON, STRAWBERRY, BANANA, MANGO)

CRACKED ICE

GARNISH

LEMON WHEEL

Method

Blend all ingredients with ice. Pour into salt-frosted glass. Serve garnished with wheel of lemon.

Martini

Ingredients

GLASS

3 oz/90mL COCKTAIL GLASS

MIXERS

1½ oz/45mL GIN

⅔ oz/20mL DRY VERMOUTH

ICE CUBES

GARNISH

twist OF LEMON RIND OR OLIVE

Method

Stir all ingredients over ice and strain. Garnish with lemon twist or olive on toothpick in the glass.

Comments: The classically sophisticated black-tie cocktail. Always stirred. However, when shaken it is known as a 'Bradford'. An olive garnish retains the gin sting whereas a lemon twist makes the cocktail smoother.

Variations: A 'Dry Martini' has less Vermouth.

Ménage à Trois

Ingredients

GLASS

10 oz/285mL HURRICANE GLASS

MIXERS

1 oz/30mL PERNOD

1 oz/30mL MALIBU

2 oz/60mL PINEAPPLE JUICE

½ oz/15mL COCONUT CREAM

1 scoop ORANGE SHERBET

1 scoop VANILLA ICE CREAM

ICE CUBES

GARNISH

1 STRAWBERRY

PINEAPPLE LEAVES

Method

Blend and pour into glass. Garnish with a strawberry, pineapple leaves and three straws.

Comments: Voulez vous coucher avec moi ce soir? When two's not enough company try this drink that originated from the afternoon cocktail parties held on the crowded houseboats lining the River Seine in Paris. Ideal for three people.

Mexican Flag

Ingredients

GLASS

5 oz/140mL CHAMPAGNE SAUCER

MIXERS

2 oz/60mL TEQUILA

$^1/_3$ oz/10mL SUGAR SYRUP

$^1/_3$ oz/10mL LIME JUICE

ICE CUBES

GARNISH

1 GREEN COCKTAIL ONION

1 WHITE COCKTAIL ONION

1 RED CHERRY

ICE CUBES

Method

Shake all ingredients over ice and pour into glass. Garnish with green and white cocktail onions and a red cherry across the glass on a toothpick.

Mexican Runner

Ingredients

GLASS

10 oz/285mL FANCY COCKTAIL GLASS

MIXERS

1 oz/30mL TEQUILA

$^1/_2$ oz/15mL TIA MARIA

$^1/_2$ oz/15mL GRAND MARNIER

$^1/_2$ oz/15mL BLACKBERRY LIQUEUR

1 oz/30mL LEMON JUICE

$^1/_2$ BANANA

2 STRAWBERRIES

CRACKED ICE

GARNISH

1 STRAWBERRY

Method

Blend all over ice and pour into glass. Garnish with a strawberry and umbrella parasol.

Midnight Sax

Ingredients

GLASS

12 oz/340mL TUMBLER GLASS

MIXERS

1 oz/30mL MIDORI MELON LIQUEUR

1 oz/30mL SOUTHERN COMFORT

1 oz/30mL ORANGE AND MANGO FRUIT JUICES

GINGER ALE

ICE CUBES

GARNISH

ORANGE SLICE

twist OF ORANGE RIND

Method

Pour all ingredients except ginger ale into glass over ice and stir, then top up with ginger ale. Garnish with slices of orange in the glass and orange twist on the side.

Comments: Jazz is the music of the moods. Experience this fiery, and soulful music with this unique cocktail, rumoured to be one of Charlie Parker's former favorites.

Midori Illusion

Ingredients

GLASS

5 oz/145mL COCKTAIL GLASS

MIXERS

1 oz/30mL MIDORI MELON LIQUEUR

1/2 oz/15mL COINTREAU

1/2 oz/15mL VODKA

1 1/2 oz/45mL LEMON JUICE

1/2 oz/15mL LIME CORDIAL OR SUGAR SYRUP

ICE CUBES

GARNISH

LIME WHEEL

Method

Shake all ingredients with ice and strain into glass. Serve garnished with lime wheel.

Midori Pash

Ingredients

GLASS

9 oz/270mL FOOTED HI-BALL GLASS

MIXERS

2 oz/60mL MIDORI MELON LIQUEUR

1 oz/30mL VODKA

1/2 oz/15mL LIME CORDIAL

CRANBERRY JUICE

ICE CUBES

GARNISH

ORANGE WHEEL

Method

Shake ingredients and strain into glass over ice. Serve garnished with wheel of orange.

Midori Splice

Ingredients

GLASS

9 oz/270mL HI-BALL GLASS

MIXERS

1 oz/30mL MIDORI MELON LIQUEUR

1 oz/30mL MALIBU

PINEAPPLE JUICE

½ oz/15mL FRESH CREAM

ICE CUBES

GARNISH

PINEAPPLE WEDGE

Method

Build Midori, Malibu and juice over ice. Float in cream.

Comments: A Midori Splice can also be served in a tulip glass.

Mint Julep

Ingredients

GLASS

10 oz/285mL HI-BALL TOM COLLINS GLASS

MIXERS

1 teaspoon SUGAR

2–3 dashes COLD WATER OR SODA WATER

5 sprigs FRESH MINT

2 oz/60mL BOURBON

CRUSHED OR SHAVED ICE

GARNISH

3 MINT SPRIGS, SUGAR-FROSTED

Method

Muddle sugar, water and 5 mint sprigs in a glass. Pour into thoroughly chilled glass and pack with ice. Add bourbon and mix with a chopping motion using a long-handled bar spoon. Garnish with remaining mint and serve with a straw.

Comments: Tear mint leaves slightly before frosting in sugar for greater aroma and flavor.

Monte Carlo

Ingredients

GLASS

3 oz/90mL COCKTAIL GLASS

MIXERS

1 oz/30mL CANADIAN CLUB RYE WHISKY

$\frac{1}{3}$ oz/10mL BENEDICTINE

2 dashes ANGOSTURA BITTERS

ICE CUBES

Method

Shake all ingredients with ice and strain into glass.

Morning Glory

Ingredients

GLASS

5 oz/145mL OLD FASHIONED SPIRIT GLASS

MIXERS

1 oz/30mL GRANT'S SCOTCH WHISKY

1 oz/30mL BRANDY

1 teaspoon PERNOD

1 teaspoon WHITE CURAÇAO

2 dashes ANGOSTURA BITTERS

SODA WATER

ICE CUBES

GARNISH

1 twist ORANGE RIND

Method

Shake all ingredients except soda water with ice and pour then top up with soda water. Garnish with orange twist.

Moscow Mule

Ingredients

GLASS

10 oz/285mL HI-BALL GLASS

MIXERS

1 oz/30mL VODKA

$\frac{1}{2}$ oz/15mL LIME CORDIAL

GINGER BEER

ICE CUBES

GARNISH

1 LEMON SLICE

1 MINT SPRIG

Method

Build in glass over ice. Garnish with a slice of lemon and mint, straws and a swizzle stick.

M cocktails

Mount Fuji

Ingredients

GLASS

3 oz/90mL COCKTAIL GLASS

MIXERS

1 oz/30mL GIN

½ oz/15mL LEMON JUICE

⅓ oz/10mL HEAVY CREAM

1 EGG WHITE

ICE CUBES

GARNISH

RED CHERRY

Method

Shake all ingredients with ice and strain into glass. Serve garnished with a red cherry.

Napoleon Seduction

Ingredients

GLASS

8 oz/230mL FOOTED HI-BALL GLASS

MIXERS

½ oz/15mL MANGO LIQUEUR

1 oz/30mL CREAM

1 oz/30mL MANDARIN NAPOLEON

½ MANGO

½ oz/15mL SABRA

CRACKED ICE

GARNISH

1 MARASCHINO CHERRY

ORANGE WHEEL

Method

Blend all the ingredients with ice until smooth. Pour into a glass. Garnish with cherry and orange wheel, and serve.

Natasha

Ingredients

GLASS

3 oz/90mL COCKTAIL GLASS

MIXERS

$1/2$ oz/15mL PEAR BRANDY

1 dash ORANGE BITTERS

$1/2$ oz/15mL APRICOT BRANDY

$1/2$ oz/15mL SWEET VERMOUTH

CRACKED ICE

GARNISH

1 MARASCHINO CHERRY

Method

Shake all ingredients and strain into glass. Garnish with cherry and serve.

cocktails

Naughty Nuptial

Ingredients

GLASS

8 oz/230mL FANCY COCKTAIL GLASS

MIXERS

1 oz/30mL TIA MARIA

½ BANANA

½ oz/15mL JAMAICAN RUM

2 oz/60mL ORANGE JUICE

2 oz/60mL PINEAPPLE JUICE

CRACKED ICE

GARNISH

1 PINEAPPLE WEDGE

PINEAPPLE LEAVES

1 CHERRY

Method

Blend all ingredients until smooth and pour into glass. Garnish with pineapple wedge, pineapple leaves and cherry, to serve.

New Yorker

Ingredients

GLASS

3 oz/90mL COCKTAIL
GLASS

MIXERS

$\frac{1}{2}$ oz/15mL GIN

1 dash COINTREAU

1$\frac{1}{2}$ oz/45mL DRY VERMOUTH

CRACKED ICE

$\frac{1}{2}$ oz/15mL SWEET SHERRY

GARNISH

ORANGE RIND

Method

Stir all ingredients in mixing
glass and strain into glass
to serve.

Night of Passion

Ingredients

GLASS
9 oz/270mL FANCY ROCKS GLASS

MIXERS
2 oz/60mL GIN

½ oz/15mL LEMON JUICE

1 oz/30mL COINTREAU

2 oz/60mL PASSIONFRUIT JUICE

2 oz/60mL PEACH NECTAR

CRACKED ICE

Method

Shake all ingredients and strain into glass to serve.

NOAH'S ARK

Ingredients

GLASS

1⅓ oz/40mL CORDIAL GLASS
(LEXINGTON)

MIXERS

⅓ oz/10mL BLUE CURAÇAO

⅓ oz/10mL CREAM

⅓ oz/10mL 7-UP

GARNISH

½ LYCHEE NUT (OPTIONAL)

Method

Shake Blue Curaçao with
cream, then float in 7-up.
Optionally, place half a lychee
nut in glass before pouring.

Norman Conquest

Ingredients

GLASS

3 oz/90mL FANCY COCKTAIL GLASS

MIXERS

2 oz/60mL CALVADOS

1 teaspoon GRENADINE CORDIAL

2 tablespoon LEMON JUICE

CRACKED ICE

GARNISH

1 LIME WHEEL

Method

Shake all ingredients and strain into glass. Serve garnished with lime wheel.

Nutcracker

Ingredients

GLASS

8 oz/230mL HI-BALL GLASS

MIXERS

1 oz/30mL FRANGELICO

1 oz/30mL DARK RUM

2 oz/60mL CLOUDY APPLE JUICE

⅓ oz/10mL FRESH LIME JUICE

1 dash ANGOSTURA BITTERS

6 MINT LEAVES

CRACKED ICE

GARNISH

1 APPLE SLICE

1 MINT SPRIG

Method

Shake all ingredients and strain over ice into glass. Garnish with an apple slice and a mint sprig.

Nutty Buddy

Ingredients

GLASS

1 1/2 oz/45mL TALL DUTCH
CORDIAL GLASS

MIXERS

1/2 oz/15mL KAHLÚA

1/2 oz/15mL CRÈME DE MENTHE

1/2 oz/15mL FRANGELICO

Method

Layer in order.

Comment: Customers should
shoot back this crazy cocktail.

Nutty Irishman

Ingredients

GLASS

IRISH COFFEE GLASS

MIXERS

1 oz/30mL
FRANGELICO

1 oz/30mL BAILEYS
IRISH CREAM

2 oz/60mL CREAM

GARNISH

CHOCOLATE FLAKES

Method

Shake all ingredients
into glass and strain.
Serve garnished with
chocolate flakes.

Oatmeal Cookie

Ingredients

GLASS

3 oz/90mL COCKTAIL GLASS

MIXERS

1 oz/30mL JÄGERMEISTER

½ oz/15mL BAILEYS IRISH CREAM

½ oz/15mL BUTTERSCOTCH SCHNAPPS

1 oz/30mL CREAM

ICE CUBES

GARNISH

CHOCOLATE SPRINKLES

Method

Shake all ingredients with ice and strain into glass. Serve garnished with chocolate sprinkles.

Oceanic

Ingredients

GLASS

5 oz/145mL CHAMPAGNE FLUTE

MIXERS

1½ oz/45mL GRANT'S SCOTCH WHISKY

½ oz/15mL BIANCO VERMOUTH

30mL KAHLÚA

CRACKED ICE

GARNISH

1 ORANGE RIND

Method

Mix all ingredients in a mixing glass and strain into champagne flute. Garnish with a spiral of orange peel and serve.

Off the Leash

Ingredients

GLASS

5 oz/145mL CHAMPAGNE SAUCER

MIXERS

3 oz/90mL BRANDY

1 oz/30mL SWEET VERMOUTH

CRACKED ICE

GARNISH

3 MARASCHINO CHERRIES

Method

Mix all ingredients in a mixing glass and strain into glass. Garnish with maraschino cherries and serve.

Old-Fashioned Appetizer

Ingredients

GLASS

5 oz/145mL OLD FASHIONED
SPIRIT GLASS

MIXERS

1 CUBE OF ICE

$^2/_3$ oz/20mL BOURBON

$^2/_3$ oz/20mL DUBONNET

1 teaspoon COINTREAU

1 teaspoon PERNOD

1 dash ANGOSTURA
BITTERS

GARNISH

LEMON RIND

ORANGE RIND

Method

Build over ice. Garnish with
lemon and orange rind.

Old-Fashioned Scotch

Ingredients

GLASS

10 oz/285mL OLD FASHIONED SPIRIT GLASS

MIXERS

1 oz/30mL GRANT'S SCOTCH WHISKY

1 dash ANGOSTURA BITTERS

SUGAR CUBE

SODA WATER

GARNISH

½ slice ORANGE

½ slice LEMON

1 CHERRY

Method

Build scotch and bitters over ice and sugar cubes. Top up with soda water. Garnish with ½ slice of orange and lemon and cherry. A swizzle stick may be used.

Comment: The origin of this cocktail is uncertain, however, some say it was invented at the Pendennis Club, Louisville, Kentucky, in the 1880s, as the result of the bar staff being asked for a 'good old fashioned cocktail'.

cocktails

Orangutan

Ingredients

GLASS

9 oz/270mL FANCY COCKTAIL
GLASS

MIXERS

1 oz/30mL MIDORI MELON
LIQUEUR

3 oz/90mL ORANGE JUICE

1 oz/30mL MANDARIN
NAPOLEON

3 oz/90mL PINEAPPLE
JUICE

CRACKED ICE

GARNISH

2 ORANGE SLICES

PINEAPPLE LEAVES

Method

Half fill a cocktail glass with ice
and build ingredients. Garnish
with orange slices, pineapple
leaves and straws to serve.

Orgasm

Ingredients

GLASS

7 oz/200mL OLD FASHIONED
SPIRIT GLASS

MIXERS

1 oz/30mL BAILEYS IRISH
CREAM

1 oz/30mL COINTREAU

ICE CUBES

GARNISH

STRAWBERRY OR
CHERRIES

Method

Build over ice.

Comments: Probably the most
widely drunk cocktail in Australia
and very popular with women.

Variations: A 'Multiple Orgasm'
is made with the addition of
1 oz/30mL of fresh
cream or milk.

A 'Screaming Multiple
Orgasm' has the
addition of ½ oz/15mL
Galliano along with
1 oz/30mL fresh cream
or milk.

Oriental Blossom

Ingredients

GLASS

8 oz/230mL COLADA GLASS

MIXERS

1 oz/30mL BANANA LIQUEUR

3 oz/90mL APPLE JUICE

1 oz/30mL SOUTHERN COMFORT

1 oz/30mL FRESH CREAM

$\frac{1}{2}$ oz/15mL RED CURAÇAO

2 APPLE SLICES

ICE CUBES

GARNISH

APPLE SLICES

Method

Shake all ingredients with ice and strain into glass. Garnish with apple slices and serve.

Oriental Pearl

Ingredients

GLASS

5 oz/145mL CHAMPAGNE SAUCER

MIXERS

$^2/_3$ oz/20mL WHITE RUM

$^1/_2$ oz/15mL FRESH CREAM

$^1/_3$ oz/10mL CRÈME DE CASSIS

CRACKED ICE

$^1/_2$ oz/15mL COLA SYRUP

GARNISH

MINT SPRIG

Method

Shake with ice and strain into glass. Serve garnished with mint sprig.

Pablo

Ingredients

GLASS

5 oz/145mL COCKTAIL GLASS

MIXERS

1 oz/30mL
BACARDI RUM

$\frac{1}{2}$ oz/15mL COINTREAU

$\frac{1}{2}$ oz/15mL ADVOCAAT

CRACKED ICE

GARNISH

1 slice PINEAPPLE

1 MARASCHINO CHERRY

Method

Shake all ingredients with ice and strain into glass. Garnish with pineapple and cherry to serve.

Pago Pago

Ingredients

GLASS

8 oz/230mL OLD FASHIONED
SPIRIT GLASS

MIXERS

½ oz/30mL BACARDI GOLD RUM

⅓ oz/10mL LIME JUICE

⅓ oz/10mL PINEAPPLE JUICE

1 teaspoon GREEN CHARTREUSE

1 teaspoon COINTREAU

ICE CUBES

GARNISH

1 PINEAPPLE WEDGE

1 CHERRY

Method

Shake all ingredients with
ice and strain into glass over
3 cubes of ice. Garnish with
a pineapple wedge and a
cherry to serve

Palm Sundae

Ingredients

GLASS

10 oz/285mL HURRICANE GLASS

MIXERS

1½ oz/45mL PEACH LIQUEUR

1 oz/30mL MALIBU

½ oz/15mL BANANA LIQUEUR

2 oz/60mL TROPICAL FRUIT JUICE

3 FRESH STRAWBERRIES

CRACKED ICE

GARNISH

1 ORANGE WEDGE

2 PINEAPPLE LEAVES

1 MARASCHINO CHERRY

Method

Blend all ingredients with ice and pour into glass. Garnish with orange wedge, pineapple leaves and maraschino cherry.

Comments: The peach flavor is exquisite in this specially designed cocktail recipe. The succulent peach liqueur is another member of the new generation of natural tropical fruit cocktails.

Papaya Sling

Ingredients

GLASS

10 oz/285mL HI-BALL GLASS

MIXERS

1 oz/30mL GIN

$^{1}/_{2}$ oz/15mL LIME JUICE

$^{2}/_{3}$ oz/20mL PAPAYA JUICE OR SYRUP

2 dashes ANGOSTURA BITTERS

SODA WATER

CRACKED ICE

GARNISH

LIME WHEEL

Method

Shake all ingredients with ice and pour into glass. Then top up with soda water. Garnish with a lime wheel.

Peach Almond Shake

Ingredients

GLASS

10 oz/285mL POCO GRANDE
GLASS

MIXERS

2 oz/60mL PEACH LIQUEUR

1 WHOLE PEELED PEACH

1 oz/30mL AMARETTO DI
GALLIANO

2 scoops VANILLA ICE CREAM

7-UP

CRACKED ICE

GARNISH

1 PEACH SLICE

SLIVERED ALMONDS

Method

Blend all ingredients with ice
and pour into glass. Then top
up with 7-up. Garnish
with a peach slice,
almonds and a straw.

Peppermint Breeze

Ingredients

GLASS

10 oz/285mL HI-BALL GLASS

MIXERS

2 oz/60mL GRANT'S SCOTCH WHISKY

FRESHLY SQUEEZED JUICE OF 1 LIME QUARTER

SODA WATER

BROWN SUGAR LUMP INFUSED WITH 4 DROPS PEPPERMINT ESSENCE

CRACKED ICE

GARNISH

FRESH MINT

Method

Build with cracked ice and add freshly squeezed lime juice. Top up with soda water and stir well. Serve garnished with fresh mint.

Comments: The fresh and reviving flavors of peppermint and lime mixed with the rich, honeyed taste of Grant's Scotch Whisky create a delicious, invigorating drink.

Picadilly Punch

Ingredients

GLASS

3 oz/90mL COCKTAIL GLASS, PREHEATED

MIXERS

1 oz/30mL COGNAC

$\frac{1}{3}$ oz/10mL SUGAR

$\frac{1}{2}$ oz/15mL LEMON JUICE

1 clove CINNAMON STICK

GROUND NUTMEG

GARNISH

1 ORANGE SLICE

1 RED CHERRY

Method

Simmer all ingredients except for Cognac. Pour Cognac into ladle and ignite before mixing into the punch mix. Stir and pour into preheated glass. Serve garnished with an orange slice and a red cherry.

Picasso

Ingredients

GLASS

3 oz/90mL COCKTAIL GLASS

MIXERS

1 oz/30mL COGNAC

$\frac{1}{3}$ oz/10mL DUBONNET

$\frac{1}{3}$ oz/10mL LIME JUICE

$\frac{1}{2}$ oz/15mL SUGAR SYRUP

ICE CUBES

GARNISH

1 twist ORANGE RIND

Method

Shake all ingredients over ice
and strain into glass. Garnish
with orange twist.

Pimm's No. 1 Cup

Ingredients

GLASS

10 oz/285mL HI-BALL GLASS

MIXERS

1–1$\frac{1}{2}$ oz/30–45mL PIMM'S NO. 1 CUP

7-UP OR DRY GINGER ALE

ICE CUBES

GARNISH

ORANGE SLICE

CHERRY

CUCUMBER (SKIN ON)

Method

Build Pimm's over ice. Top-up with either 7-up or dry ginger or equal parts of both. Garnish with an orange slice, cherry, cucumber skin, swizzle stick and straws.

Comments: A slice of orange can detract from the sweet aftertaste. Slicing the inside of the cucumber skin allows the small drops to keep the drink chilled. Originally six types of Pimm's were commonly consumed, today there are only two: Pimm's No.1, which has a gin base, and Pimm's No. 2, which has a vodka base. Often referred to as the 'Fruit Cocktail Cocktail'.

Pina Colada

Ingredients

GLASS

10 oz/285mL HI-BALL GLASS

MIXERS

1 oz/30mL BACARDI RUM

1 oz/30mL COCONUT CREAM

1 oz/30mL SUGAR SYRUP

4 oz/125mL UNSWEETENED
PINEAPPLE JUICE

ICE CUBES

GARNISH

1 PINEAPPLE WEDGE

3 PINEAPPLE LEAVES

Method

Shake all ingredients with ice
and pour into glass. Garnish
with a pineapple wedge,
pineapple leaves, straws and
swizzle stick.

Comments: A tropical Hawaiian
cocktail which is distinguished
by including coconut cream.

Pineapple Plantation

Ingredients

GLASS

10 oz/285mL FOOTED HI-BALL GLASS

MIXERS

1 oz/30mL AMARETTO DI GALLIANO

1 oz/30mL SOUTHERN COMFORT

3 oz/90mL PINEAPPLE JUICE

7-UP

CRACKED ICE

GARNISH

1 PINEAPPLE WEDGE

1 CHERRY

Method

Blend all ingredients except 7-up with ice and pour into glass. Then top up with 7-up. Garnish with pineapple wedge and cherry.

Pink Gin

Ingredients

GLASS

10 oz/285mL HURRICANE GLASS

MIXERS

3 dashes ANGOSTURA BITTERS

2 ICE CUBES

1½ oz/45mL GIN

1 oz/30mL WATER

GARNISH

1 LEMON SLICE

1 CHERRY

Method

Put bitters into glass. Rotate in the glass, then throw out the bitters. Add ice cubes, gin and water, and serve.

Pink Panther

Ingredients

GLASS

5 oz/145mL CHAMPAGNE
SAUCER

MIXERS

²/₃ oz/20mL BOURBON

1 oz/30mL VODKA

¹/₂ oz/15mL MALIBU

1¹/₂ oz/45mL CREAM

1 dash GRENADINE CORDIAL

GARNISH

1 CHERRY

MINT LEAF

Method

Shake all ingredients with ice
and strain into glass. Garnish
with cherry and mint.

Polynesia

Ingredients

GLASS

5 oz/145mL TULIP CHAMPAGNE
FLUTE

MIXERS

1 oz/30mL BACARDI RUM

1 oz/30mL PASSIONFRUIT
LIQUEUR OR $\frac{1}{2}$ PASSIONFRUIT

$\frac{1}{3}$ oz/10mL LIME JUICE

$\frac{1}{2}$ EGG WHITE

CRACKED ICE

GARNISH

PASSIONFRUIT

Method

Blend all ingredients with ice
and pour into glass. Garnish
with passionfruit.

Prairie Oyster

Ingredients

GLASS

3 oz/90mL COCKTAIL GLASS

MIXERS

1 oz/30mL BRANDY

SALT AND PEPPER

1 dash WORCESTERSHIRE SAUCE

1 dash TABASCO SAUCE

1 EGG YOLK

Method

Build ingredients in order, no ice.

Comments: The spices relieve a sore head and the brandy replenishes lost energy. Brandy may be replaced with any spirit of your choice, however cold vodka is medically soothing. Best before breakfast.

Pretty Woman

Ingredients

GLASS
10 oz/285mL HURRICANE GLASS

MIXERS – BLEND 1
1 oz/30mL MIDORI MELON
LIQUEUR

1 oz/30mL MALIBU

MIXERS – BLEND 2
1 oz/30mL STRAWBERRY
LIQUEUR

3–4 STRAWBERRIES

CRACKED ICE

GARNISH
1 STRAWBERRY

Method

Blend with ice in two separate
blenders and pour into glass.
Tilt the glass when pouring the
two sets of ingredients into the
glass. Garnish with strawberry
and umbrella to serve.

GARNISH

1 ORANGE SLICE

Method

Shake all ingredients except
Champagne with ice and strain.
Then top up with Champagne.
Garnish with orange slice.

Prince of Wales

Ingredients

GLASS

5 oz/145mL CHAMPAGNE
SAUCER

MIXERS

½ oz/15mL MADEIRA

½ oz/15mL BRANDY

1 teaspoon COINTREAU

1–2 dashes ANGOSTURA
BITTERS

CHAMPAGNE

ICE CUBES

Puerto Rican Pink Lady

Ingredients

GLASS

5 oz/145mL TULIP CHAMPAGNE FLUTE, SUGAR-FROSTED

MIXERS

1 oz/30mL BACARDI GOLD RUM

⅓ oz/10mL LEMON JUICE

⅓ oz/10mL GRENADINE CORDIAL

½ EGG WHITE

CRACKED ICE

GARNISH

1 STRAWBERRY

Method

Blend all ingredients with ice and pour into glass. Garnish with a strawberry splashed with Grenadine.

Puerto Rico Rickey (picture on cover)

Ingredients

GLASS

10 oz/285mL HI-BALL GLASS

MIXERS

2 oz/60mL GIN

1 oz/30mL LIME JUICE

ICE CUBES

2 dashes RASPBERRY SYRUP

SODA WATER

GARNISH

LIME WHEEL

Method

Pour gin and lime juice over ice into glass. Add the raspberry syrup and top up with soda water. Garnish with a wheel of lime to serve.

Comments: Bourbon, rum or whisky can be substituted for gin.

Purple People Eater

Ingredients

GLASS

3 oz/90mL COCKTAIL GLASS

MIXERS

1 oz/30mL PARFAIT AMOUR

1 oz/30mL GIN

1 teaspoon LEMON JUICE

ICE CUBES

GARNISH

1 STRAWBERRY

Method

Shake all ingredients over ice and strain into glass. Garnish with a strawberry and pink parasol to serve.

QF

Ingredients

GLASS

SHOT GLASS

MIXERS

⅓ oz/10mL KAHLÚA

⅓ oz/10mL MIDORI MELON
LIQUEUR

⅓ oz/10mL BAILEYS IRISH
CREAM

Method

Layer in order.

Queens

GLASS

5 oz/145mL TULIP CHAMPAGNE FLUTE

MIXERS

1 oz/30mL DRY GIN

1 oz/30mL PINEAPPLE JUICE

1 oz/30mL DRY VERMOUTH

1 oz/30mL SWEET VERMOUTH (BIANCO)

CRACKED ICE

GARNISH

1 MARASCHINO CHERRY

1 PINEAPPLE WEDGE

Method

Shake all ingredients with ice and strain into glass. Garnish with cherry, pineapple wedge to serve.

R&R

Ingredients

GLASS

3 oz/90mL FANCY COCKTAIL GLASS

MIXERS

1 oz/30mL COINTREAU

1 oz/30mL MIDORI MELON LIQUEUR

1 oz/30mL TEQUILA

Method

Layer in order in glass and serve.

Rabbit's Revenge

Ingredients

5 oz/145mL FANCY COCKTAIL
GLASS

MIXERS

1½ oz/45mL BOURBON

3 dashes GRENADINE CORDIAL

1 oz/30mL PINEAPPLE JUICE

CRACKED ICE

TONIC WATER

GARNISH

1 ORANGE SLICE

Method

Shake ingredients except tonic
water and strain into a tumbler
glass. Top up with tonic water
and garnish with orange slice
to serve.

Rainbow Sherbet

Ingredients

GLASS

7 oz/200mL TULIP CHAMPAGNE FLUTE

MIXERS

½ oz/15mL MIDORI MELON LIQUEUR

½ oz/15mL BANANA LIQUEUR

½ oz/15mL STRAWBERRY LIQUEUR

2 oz/60mL ORANGE JUICE

2 dashes GRENADINE CORDIAL

2 scoops ORANGE SHERBET

GARNISH

ASSORTED FRUIT

BLUE FOOD COLORING

Method

Blend all ingredients without ice. Pour into glass. Garnish with assorted fruit and a dash of blue food coloring.

Ramona

Ingredients

GLASS

10 oz/285mL HI-BALL GLASS

MIXERS

2 oz/60mL BACARDI RUM

2 teaspoons CASTER SUGAR

1 oz/30mL COINTREAU

2 oz/60mL LEMON JUICE

CRACKED ICE

SODA WATER

GARNISH

1 LEMON WHEEL

Method

Shake all ingredients except soda water and strain over ice into glass. Top up with soda water, garnish with lemon wheel and straws to serve.

Red Eye

Ingredients

GLASS

10 oz/285mL HI-BALL GLASS

MIXERS

5 oz/145mL COLD BEER

5 oz/145mL TOMATO JUICE

GARNISH

$^1/_2$ CHERRY TOMATO

Method

Pour tomato juice into glass, add beer and serve.

Reflections

Ingredients

GLASS

3 oz/90mL MARTINI
GLASS

MIXERS

1 oz/30mL FRANGELICO
CRACKED ICE

1 oz/30mL WHITE CRÈME DE
CACAO

$\frac{1}{2}$ oz/15mL CHERI-SUISSE

GARNISH

2 MARASCHINO CHERRIES

1 RED STRAW

Method

Shake all ingredients into ice
and strain into glass. Cut $\frac{1}{4}$ in/
5mm off a red straw and use it
to join two maraschino cherries.
Place one of the cherries in the
glass and the other above the
liquid, creating a reflection
effect, and serve.

cocktails

Rhett Butler

Ingredients

GLASS

10 oz/285mL HI-BALL GLASS

MIXERS

1 oz/30mL SOUTHERN COMFORT

1 teaspoon LIME CORDIAL

1 oz/30mL ORANGE CURAÇAO

½ oz/15mL LEMON JUICE

SODA WATER

CRACKED ICE

GARNISH

1 ORANGE WHEEL

Method

Build all ingredients except soda water over ice in a hi-ball glass, top up with soda water. Garnish with orange wheel and serve with straws.

Rolls Royce

Ingredients

GLASS

3 oz/90mL FANCY COCKTAIL GLASS

MIXERS

1 oz/30mL DRY GIN

⅓ oz/10mL BENEDICTINE

½ oz/15mL DRY VERMOUTH

½ oz/15mL SWEET VERMOUTH (BIANCO)

CRACKED ICE

Method

Stir all ingredients, strain into glass, and serve.

Roman Driver

Ingredients

GLASS

5 oz/145mL CHAMPAGNE SAUCER

MIXERS

1 oz/30mL
GALLIANO
LIQUEUR

1 dash GRENADINE CORDIAL

½ oz/15mL VODKA

⅔ oz/20mL FRESH CREAM

⅔ oz/20mL ALMOND SYRUP

CRACKED ICE

GARNISH

1 twist ORANGE RIND

Method

Shake all ingredients.
Strain into champagne
saucer and serve garnished
with twist of orange rind.

MIXERS

1 oz/30mL BRANDY

2 oz/60mL GRAPEFRUIT JUICE

2 oz/60mL COINTREAU

1/3 oz/10mL GRENADINE CORDIAL

SPARKLING WHITE WINE

CRACKED ICE

Royal Flush

Ingredients

GLASS

8 oz/230mL TUMBLER GLASS

Method

Shake all ingredients except sparkling wine and strain into glass, top up with wine and serve with straws.

Rum Rebellion

Ingredients

GLASS

7 oz/200mL OLD FASHIONED
SPIRIT GLASS

MIXERS

1 oz/30mL BACARDI RUM

1 teaspoon CHERRY BRANDY

1 oz/30mL BANANA LIQUEUR

2½ oz/75mL PINEAPPLE JUICE

1 scoop CRUSHED ICE

GARNISH

PINEAPPLE WEDGE

Method

Blend ingredients until smooth
and pour into a glass. Serve
garnished with pineapple wedge.

Running Hot

Ingredients

GLASS

7 oz/200mL OLD FASHIONED
SPIRIT GLASS

MIXERS

1½ oz/45mL BACARDI RUM

1½ oz/45mL PINEAPPLE JUICE

1 oz/30mL COINTREAU

1 dash GRENADINE CORDIAL

ICE CUBES

Method

Shake all ingredients and strain
over ice into glass and serve.

Russian Holiday

Ingredients

GLASS

10 oz/285mL HI-BALL GLASS

MIXERS

1 oz/30mL VODKA

2 oz/60mL PINEAPPLE JUICE

⅔ oz/20mL GRAND MARNIER

1 oz/30mL WHIPPED CREAM (FLOAT)

CRACKED ICE

Method

Pour vodka and pineapple juice over ice into glass. Float whipped cream, add Grand Marnier and serve.

Russian Roulette

Ingredients

BRANDY BALLOON

MIXERS

$^1/_2$ oz/15mL GALLIANO LIQUEUR

$^1/_3$ oz/10mL SUGAR SYRUP

$^1/_2$ oz/15mL BANANA LIQUEUR

$^1/_2$ BANANA

$^1/_2$ oz/15mL VODKA

$^1/_2$ oz/15mL LEMON JUICE

1 oz/30mL ORANGE JUICE

1 scoop CRUSHED ICE

GARNISH

1 STRAWBERRY

Method

Blend all ingredients until smooth. Pour into a brandy balloon to serve.

Rusty Spade

Ingredients

GLASS

10 oz/285mL FANCY COCKTAIL
GLASS

MIXERS

1 MANGO

1 oz/30mL STRAWBERRY
LIQUEUR

1 PASSIONFRUIT

FRESH CREAM

ICE CUBES

GARNISH

1 STRAWBERRY

Method

Blend all ingredients with
ice. Serve garnished with
strawberry fan on side of glass.

Sail Away

Ingredients

GLASS

5 oz/145mL COCKTAIL GLASS

MIXERS

1 oz/30mL MIDORI MELON LIQUEUR

1 oz/30mL LIME JUICE

$^{1}/_{2}$ oz/15mL PEACH LIQUEUR

1 dash LEMON JUICE

30mL VODKA

ICE CUBES

GARNISH

1 LIME WHEEL

Method

Shake all ingredients with ice and strain into glass. Garnish with lime wheel to serve.

Salty Dog

Ingredients

GLASS

10 oz/285mL HI-BALL GLASS,
SALT-FROSTED

MIXERS

1 oz/30mL VODKA

1 oz/30mL SUGAR SYRUP

GRAPEFRUIT JUICE

ICE CUBES

Method

Shake all ingredients and pour
into glass over ice.

Comments: When drinking, don't
use a straw – drink straight from
the salt-frosted glass.

Sambuca Shaker

Ingredients

GLASS

WINE GLASS

MIXERS

1 oz/30mL SAMBUCA

Method

Pour Sambuca into glass then light. Cup your hand entirely over the rim while it flames, creating suction. Shake the glass, place under your nose, take hand from glass to inhale the fumes, then shoot.

Comments: Everybody shakes to this latest fad. The wider the rim the easier the suction.

Sangria

Ingredients

GLASS

RED WINE GLASS

MIXERS

ORANGE PIECES, LIME PIECES, LEMON PIECES, STRAWBERRY PIECES SOAKED IN SUGAR SYRUP

SPANISH RED WINE

1 oz/30mL COINTREAU

1 oz/30mL BRANDY

1 oz/30mL BACARDI RUM

Method

Pour in order.

Comments: Thinly slice orange and lime and place in bowl. Pour in sugar syrup and allow to stand for several hours. Add red wine into glass until half full and add other ingredients.

Scarlett O'Hara

Ingredients

GLASS
4 oz/130mL COCKTAIL GLASS

MIXERS
1 oz/30mL SOUTHERN COMFORT
1 oz/30mL CRANBERRY JUICE
1 teaspoon LIME JUICE
CRACKED ICE

GARNISH
1 MARASCHINO CHERRY
1 LIME SLICE

Method

Shake all ingredients with ice and strain into glass. Garnish with maraschino cherry and lime slice.

Comments: Named after the famous character from Margaret Mitchell's epic novel 'Gone with the Wind'.

Scorpion

GLASS

6 oz/170mL MARGARITA GLASS

MIXERS

$\frac{1}{2}$ oz/15mL DARK RUM

$\frac{1}{2}$ oz/15mL COGNAC

$\frac{1}{2}$ oz/15mL SAMBUCA

$\frac{1}{2}$ oz/15mL ORGEAT

$1\frac{1}{2}$ oz/45mL ORANGE JUICE

$\frac{1}{2}$ oz/15mL LEMON JUICE

CRACKED ICE

GARNISH

1 LIME WHEEL

1 CHERRY

Method

Blend all ingredients with ice and pour into glass. Garnish with a lime wheel and cherry.

Comments: The trading capital of the Middle East is where this perilous animal and cocktail comes from! Like the animal this cocktail has a sting in its tail. Orgeat is an almond-flavored non-alcoholic syrup. Amaretto may be used as a substitute.

Scotch Mist

Ingredients

GLASS

5 oz/145mL OLD FASHIONED
SPIRIT GLASS

MIXERS

1 oz/30mL GRANT'S SCOTCH
WHISKY

ICE CUBES

GARNISH

LEMON RIND

Method

Shake over ice and pour into
glass. Garnish with lemon rind.

Screwdriver

Ingredients

GLASS

7 oz/200mL OLD FASHIONED
SPIRIT GLASS

MIXERS

1 ½ oz/45mL VODKA

1 ½ oz/45mL ORANGE JUICE

ICE CUBES

GARNISH

TWIST OR SPIRAL OF ORANGE
RIND

Method

Build over ice. Serve garnished
with orange twist.

Comments: A frequently
requested mixed drink.
Suitable at any time of day.
The original recipe contains
equal measurements of vodka
and orange juice.

Variations: A Comfortable Screw
is made with 1 oz/30mL Vodka,
½ oz/15mL Southern Comfort
and topped with orange juice.

A Slow Comfortable Screw
has the addition of ½ oz/15mL
Sloe Gin.

A Long Slow Comfortable Screw
is a longer drink with more
orange juice served in a 10 oz/
285mL Hi-Ball glass.

A Long Slow Comfortable
Screw Up Against A Wall has
the addition of ½ oz/15mL
Galliano floated.

Shirley Temple

Ingredients

GLASS

10 oz/285mL HI-BALL GLASS

MIXERS

$^1/_2$ oz/15mL GRENADINE CORDIAL

GINGER ALE OR 7-UP

ICE CUBES

GARNISH

1 ORANGE SLICE

$^1/_2$ STRAWBERRY

Method

Pour Grenadine over ice. Top up with ginger ale or 7-up. Garnish with slice of orange and strawberry. Serve with swizzle stick and two straws.

Sidecar

Ingredients

GLASS

3 oz/90mL COCKTAIL GLASS

MIXERS

1 oz/30mL
BRANDY

$\frac{2}{3}$ oz/20mL
COINTREAU

1 oz/30mL LEMON JUICE

ICE CUBES

GARNISH

TWIST LEMON RIND

Method

Shake all ingredients with ice and strain. Serve garnished with lemon rind.

Comments: A zappy pre-dinner cocktail. The lemon juice purifies the brandy and ferments the Cointreau. Too much lemon juice will leave an acidic after-taste.

Singapore Sling

Ingredients

GLASS

10 oz/285mL HI-BALL GLASS

MIXERS

1 oz/30mL GIN

1 oz/30mL ORANGE JUICE

1 oz/30mL CHERRY BRANDY OR LIQUEUR

1 oz/30mL LIME JUICE

½ oz/15mL COINTREAU

1 oz/30mL PINEAPPLE JUICE

dash ANGOSTURA BITTERS

½ oz/15mL BENEDICTINE

ICE CUBES

GARNISH

1 ORANGE SLICE

1 MINT SPRIG

1 CHERRY

Method

Shake all ingredients with ice and pour into glass. Garnish with orange slice, mint, cherry, swizzle stick and straws.

Comments: This recipe is the original Singapore version. With its fruit juices it tastes totally different from other gin cocktails.

Slippery Nipple

Ingredients

GLASS

TALL DUTCH CORDIAL

MIXERS

1 oz/30mL SAMBUCA

1 oz/30mL BAILEYS IRISH
CREAM

Method

Float sambuca over Baileys into
glass and serve.

Snowball

Ingredients

GLASS

10 oz/285mL HI-BALL GLASS

MIXERS

1 oz/30mL ADVOCAAT LIQUEUR

7-UP

dash LIME CORDIAL

FRESH CREAM, OPTIONAL

GARNISH

1 RED CHERRY

Method

Build all ingredients over ice. Garnish with Red cherry, swizzle sticks and straws.

Comments: It's better to place ice in the glass after mixing the advocaat with 7-up before floating cream on top. The pressure will create the desired 'snowball' effect.

South Pacific

Ingredients

GLASS

10 oz/285mL HI-BALL GLASS

MIXERS

1 oz/30mL GIN

1/2 oz/15mL GALLIANO LIQUEUR

7-UP

1/2 oz/15mL BLUE CURAÇAO

ICE CUBES

GARNISH

1 LEMON SLICE

1 CHERRY

Method

Build gin, Galliano and 7-up over ice, then add the Blue Curaçao. Garnish with lemon slice and cherry, a swizzle stick and straws.

Comments: Australia's first gold-medal winning cocktail. Created by Gary Revell, won the World Cocktail Championships in Yugoslavia.

Soviet Cocktail

Ingredients

GLASS

3 oz/90mL COCKTAIL GLASS

MIXERS

1 oz/30mL VODKA

$^1/_3$ oz/10mL DRY VERMOUTH

$^1/_3$ oz/10mL AMONTILLADO SHERRY

ICE CUBES

GARNISH

1 twist LEMON RIND

Method

Shake all ingredients over ice and pour into glass. Garnish with a twist of lemon.

Comments: Amontillado sherry has a medium dry taste and nutty flavor. May be substituted by Amaretto.

Spanish Moss

Ingredients

GLASS

5 oz/145mL OLD FASHIONED SPIRIT GLASS

MIXERS

1 oz/30mL CHAMBORD

$\frac{1}{3}$ oz/10mL KAHLÚA

1 teaspoon GREEN CRÈME DE MENTHE

ICE CUBES

GARNISH

1 GREEN CHERRY

Method

Shake all ingredients with ice and strain over a cube of ice into glass. Garnish with a green cherry.

Comments: Chambord is a raspberry-flavored liqueur from France.

Spritzer

Ingredients

GLASS

7 oz/200mL WINE GLASS

MIXERS

DRY WHITE WINE

CHILLED SODA WATER

Method

Build, no ice.

Comments: 'Wet the whistle' with a responsible alternative. Most prefer the soda water dilution although you may prefer 7-up.

St Moritz

Ingredients

GLASS

5 oz/145mL OLD FASHIONED
SPIRIT GLASS

MIXERS

1 oz/30mL SCHNAPPS
ICE CUBES

GARNISH

HEAVY CREAM

Method

Pour into glass over ice. Float
in a layer of heavy cream.

Comments: Traditionally this
drink is made with Chambord (a
raspberry-flavored liqueur from
France) instead of schnapps.

Stars and Stripes

Ingredients

GLASS
10 oz/285mL FANCY COCKTAIL GLASS

MIXERS
⅓ oz/10mL BLUE CURAÇAO

BLEND 1
1 oz/30mL SOUTHERN COMFORT

1 oz/30mL FRANGELICO

CRACKED ICE

BLEND 2
1 oz/30mL STRAWBERRY LIQUEUR

3–4 STRAWBERRIES

CRACKED ICE

GARNISH
CHOCOLATE FLAKES

1 STRAWBERRY

Method

Pour Blue Curaçao into glass. Blend other ingredients with ice in 2 separate blenders and float in. Sprinkle chocolate flakes over top and add a strawberry and USA flag to side of glass.

Comments: Tilt the glass when pouring in the two sets of ingredients. A refreshingly super-powered alcoholic cocktail without juice.

Strawberry Blonde

Ingredients

GLASS

10 oz/285mL HI-BALL GLASS

MIXERS

1 oz/30mL DARK CRÈME DE CACAO

COLA

1 oz/30mL FRESH CREAM

dash GRENADINE CORDIAL

ICE CUBES

GARNISH

1 RED CHERRY

Method

Pour Crème de Cacao over ice. Top up with cola. Float cream on top. Garnish with red cherry, swizzle sticks and straws.

Comments: Tasting this cocktail will reveal why 'blondes have more fun'. Placing ice in the glass after mixing the cacao with cola will support the floating cream on top. A dessert cocktail, ideal on a blind date.

Sunken Treasure

Ingredients

GLASS

3 oz/90mL COCKTAIL GLASS

MIXERS

1 oz/30mL GIN

½ oz/15mL PEACH LIQUEUR

CHAMPAGNE

GARNISH

1 teaspoon APRICOT JAM

1 STRAWBERRY

Method

Stir gin and peach liqueur over ice, strain into glass and top up with Champagne. Place apricot jam in the bottom of glass and then push a strawberry into jam.

Comments: It is always pleasing to include innovative cocktail garnishes.

TNT

Ingredients

GLASS

3 oz/90mL COCKTAIL GLASS

MIXERS

1½ oz/45mL BRANDY

⅔ oz/20mL ORANGE LIQUEUR

dash PERNOD

dash ANGOSTURA BITTERS

GARNISH

ORANGE TWIST

Method

Stir all ingredients over ice and strain into glass.

Comments: A powder keg, a cocktail that will really liven up the party. Drink in moderation, as this one can really cause a 'bang'.

Tall Dutch Egg Nog

Ingredients

GLASS

10 oz/285mL BEER GLASS OR MUG

MIXERS

1 oz/30mL BACARDI RUM

1 oz/30mL ORANGE JUICE

⅓ oz/10mL DARK RUM

⅓ oz/10mL ADVOCAAT

4 oz/125mL MILK

CRACKED ICE

GARNISH

CINNAMON

EGG

Method

Blend all ingredients with ice and pour into glass. Garnish with a sprinkle of cinnamon and egg.

Tauris

Ingredients

GLASS

OLD FASHIONED GLASS SPIRIT GLASS

MIXERS

4 LIMES

MINT

RAW SUGAR AND SUGAR SYRUP

1 oz/30mL VODKA

1 oz/30mL MIDORI MELON LIQUEUR

dash CRANBERRY JUICE

ICE CUBES

Method

Muddle the limes, mint and sugar in glass. Add the remaining ingredients. Stir vigorously and serve.

_T_ cocktails

Temptation

Ingredients

GLASS

5 oz/145mL CHAMPAGNE SAUCER

MIXERS

2 oz/60mL CANADIAN CLUB RYE WHISKEY

1/2 oz/15mL DUBONNET

1/2 oz/15mL PERNOD

1/2 oz/15mL WHITE CURAÇAO

ICE CUBES

GARNISH

1 twist ORANGE RIND

Method

Stir all ingredients with ice and strain into champagne saucer. Garnish with twist of orange rind and serve.

Tennessee Sour

Ingredients

GLASS

5 oz/145mL FANCY COCKTAIL

MIXERS

2 oz/60mL JACK DANIEL'S TENNESSEE WHISKEY

JUICE ½ LEMON

½ teaspoon SUGAR

CRACKED ICE

SODA WATER

GARNISH

½ slice LEMON

1 MARASCHINO CHERRY

Method

Shake all ingredients except soda water. Strain into glass, top up with soda water. Garnish with lemon slice and cherry and serve.

Tequila Slammer

Ingredients

GLASS

7 oz/200mL OLD FASHIONED
SPIRIT GLASS

MIXERS

1 oz/30mL TEQUILA

2 oz/60mL DRY GINGER ALE

Method

Build, no ice.

Comments: A one-hit wonder - holding a coaster over the entire rim, rotate the glass clockwise on the bar 4–5 times. Lift and 'slam' the base of the glass down onto the bar, then skol in one shot. The carbonated mixer fizzes the Tequila when slammed.

Often bartenders splash in only $\frac{1}{6}$–$\frac{1}{3}$ oz/ 5–10mL of Dry Ginger Ale to aid the quick drinking process.

Tequila Sunrise

Ingredients

GLASS

10 oz/285mL HI-BALL
GLASS

MIXERS

1 oz/30mL TEQUILA

1 teaspoon GRENADINE
CORDIAL

ORANGE JUICE

GARNISH

ORANGE SLICE

Method

Build Tequila and Grenadine over
ice, then top up with orange
juice. Garnish with orange slice,
swizzle stick and straws.

Comments: Sipping this long
cool cocktail at sunrise or
sunset is magnificent. To obtain
the cleanest visual effect, drop
the Grenadine down the inside
of the glass after topping up
with orange juice. Dropping
Grenadine in the middle creates
a fallout effect, detracting from
the presentation of the cocktail.
Best served with chilled, freshly
squeezed oranges.

Tequila Sunrise No. 2

Ingredients

GLASS
5 oz/145mL FANCY COCKTAIL GLASS

MIXERS
1 oz/30mL TEQUILA

1 teaspoon LEMON JUICE

1/2 oz/15mL GALLIANO LIQUEUR

CRACKED ICE

1/2 oz/15mL BANANA LIQUEUR

1 teaspoon GRENADINE CORDIAL

GARNISH
1 ORANGE SLICE

2 MARASCHINO CHERRIES

Method

Shake all ingredients with ice and and strain into glass. Garnish with slice of orange and cherries to serve.

The Ripper

Ingredients

GLASS

3 oz/90mL CHAMPAGNE SAUCER

MIXERS

1 oz/30ml BANANA LIQUEUR

1 oz/30ml PEACHTREE LIQUEUR

$^1/_2$ oz/15ml DRY VERMOUTH

1 teaspoon BLUE CURAÇAO

$^1/_2$ oz/15ml LEMON JUICE

ICE CUBES

GARNISH

1 LEMON WHEEL

1 MINT SPRIG

Method

Shake all ingredients and strain into glass. Garnish with lemon wheel and mint sprig.

The Time Warp

Ingredients

GLASS

5 oz/145mL COCKTAIL GLASS

MIXERS

2/3 oz/20mL MIDORI
MELON LIQUEUR

1/2 oz/15mL MALIBU

CRACKED ICE

1/2 oz/15mL PINEAPPLE JUICE

GARNISH

1 teaspoon BLUE CURACAO

1 teaspoon RASPBERRY CORDIAL

2 CHERRIES

Method

Shake Midori, Malibu and pineapple juice with ice strain into glass. Add raspberry cordial and Blue Curaçao. Garnish with cherries and serve.

Three Sisters

Ingredients

GLASS

5 oz/145mL CHAMPAGNE SAUCER

MIXERS

1½ oz/45mL BRANDY

1 dash GRENADINE CORDIAL

1½ oz/45mL GALLIANO LIQUEUR

1½ oz/45mL ORANGE JUICE

CRACKED ICE

GARNISH

1 ORANGE SLICE

Method

Shake all ingredients and strain into champagne saucer, garnish with orange slice and serve.

T cocktails

Time Out

Ingredients

GLASS

8 oz/230mL
TUMBLER
GLASS

MIXERS

1 oz/30mL BRANDY

1 oz/30mL KAHLÚA

2 oz/60mL ORANGE JUICE

1 oz/30mL FRESH CREAM

1 PEACH, STONED

dash GRENADINE CORDIAL

CRACKED ICE

GARNISH

2 PINEAPPLE WEDGES

1 CANTALOUPE SLICE

Method

Blend ingredients
with ice pour
into glass. Serve
garnished with
pineapple wedge
and cantaloupe.

Tom Collins

Ingredients

GLASS

10 oz/285mL FOOTED HI-BALL
OR TOM COLLINS GLASS

MIXERS

2 oz/60mL GIN

2 oz/60mL LEMON JUICE

1 teaspoon SUGAR

CRACKED ICE

SODA WATER

GARNISH

1 MARASCHINO CHERRY

1 LEMON WHEEL

Method

Pour ingredients into glass and
top up with soda water. Garnish
with cherry, lemon wheel and
straws to serve.

Transclant

Ingredients

GLASS

10 oz/285mL FOOTED HI-BALL GLASS

MIXERS

1 oz/30mL BACARDI RUM

1 dash GALLIANO LIQUEUR

1 dash CRÈME DE MENTHE

CRACKED ICE

ORANGE JUICE

GARNISH

1 ORANGE SLICE

Method

Pour all alcohol into glass and top up with orange juice. Garnish with orange slice and straws to serve.

Triple Bypass

Ingredients

GLASS

3 oz/90mL COCKTAIL GLASS

MIXERS

²⁄₃ oz/20mL CRÈME DE CASSIS

²⁄₃ oz/20mL WHITE CRÈME DE MENTHE

²⁄₃ oz/20mL CHERRY BRANDY

1 oz/30mL FRESH CREAM

Method

Layer liqueur's in order then float in cream.

Tropical Ambrosia

Ingredients

GLASS

10 oz/285mL FOOTED HI-BALL
GLASS

MIXERS

1 MANDARIN OR ORANGE
LIQUEUR

1 APPLE

5 oz/145mL COCONUT MILK

½ oz/15mL LEMON JUICE

1 oz/30mL WHITE RUM

CRACKED ICE

GARNISH

1 APPLE SLICE

Method

Blend all ingredients with ice
and pour into glass. Garnish
with apple slice.

cocktails T

GARNISH

NUTMEG

Method

Shake all ingredients and strain into champagne saucer, sprinkle with nutmeg and serve.

Tropical Delight

Ingredients

GLASS

5 oz/145mL CHAMPAGNE SAUCER

MIXERS

1 oz/30mL DARK RUM

CRACKED ICE

1 oz/30mL CREAM

$^2/_3$ oz/20mL ORANGE JUICE

Tropical Paradise

Ingredients

GLASS

5 oz/145mL COCKTAIL GLASS

MIXERS

1½ oz/45mL BACARDI RUM

1 teaspoon LEMON JUICE

1½ oz/45mL PEACHTREE LIQUEUR

1 slice MANGO

⅔ oz/20mL MANGO LIQUEUR

1 dash MANGO NECTAR

CRACKED ICE

Method

Blend all ingredients with ice and pour into a glass and serve.

Turkish Delight

Ingredients

GLASS

14 oz/400mL COLADA GLASS

MIXERS

½ oz/30mL SABRA

1 teaspoon GRENADINE CORDIAL

½ oz/15mL PARFAIT AMOUR

CRACKED ICE

1 oz/30mL CREAM

4 oz/125mL MILK

GARNISH

CHOCOLATE FLAKES

Method

Shake all ingredients and strain into glass. Sprinkle with chocolate flakes, add straws and serve.

V-Bomb

Ingredients

GLASS

14 oz/400mL BEER GLASS

MIXERS

2 oz/60mL VODKA

½ oz/15mL LEMON JUICE

WHITE WINE

ICE CUBES

GARNISH

LEMON WHEEL

Method

Build over ice. Top up with white wine. Serve garnished with lemon wheel.

Vanilla Twist

Ingredients

GLASS

7 oz/200mL TUMBLER GLASS

MIXERS

1 oz/30mL GALLIANO VANILLA

1 oz/30mL ABSOLUT CITRON

½ oz/15mL COINTREAU

1 oz/30mL CRANBERRY JUICE

JUICE OF ½ LIME

SODA WATER

ICE CUBES

GARNISH

PINEAPPLE CHUNK

Method

Shake all ingredients except soda water. Strain into ice filled glass. Top up with soda water.

Velvet Hue

Ingredients

GLASS

7 oz/200mL FANCY COCKTAIL
GLASS

MIXERS

1 oz/30mL BRANDY

1 oz/30mL TIA MARIA

1 oz/30mL COINTREAU

2 oz/60mL CREAM

ICE CUBES

GARNISH

1 STRAWBERRY

Method

Shake all ingredients and
strain into glass. Serve
garnished with strawberry.

Vermouth Cassis

Ingredients

GLASS

8 oz/230mL FOOTED
HI-BALL GLASS

MIXERS

3 oz/90mL DRY
VERMOUTH

SODA WATER

1⅓ oz/40mL CRÈME DE
CASSIS

ICE CUBES

GARNISH

1 LEMON RIND

Method

Place a few ice cubes
in glass along with
Vermouth and Crème
de Cassis. Top up with
soda water and garnish
with lemon rind to serve.

Virgin Maria

Ingredients

GLASS

10 oz/285mL FOOTED HI-BALL
    GLASS

MIXERS

7 oz/200mL TOMATO JUICE

dash LEMON JUICE

1/2 oz/15mL CHILI SAUCE

CRACKED ICE

GARNISH

CUCUMBER SLICE

CHERRY TOMATOES

Method

Blend all ingredients with
ice and pour into glass.
Garnish with cucumber
slice, cherry tomatoes and
optional decoration.

Comments: A very hot and spicy
non-alcoholic drink, guaranteed
to get you that way.

Virgin Mary

Ingredients

GLASS

10 oz/285mL HI-BALL GLASS,
SALT-FROSTED

MIXERS

5 oz/145mL TOMATO JUICE

$^1/_2$ oz/15mL LEMON JUICE

1 teaspoon WORCESTERSHIRE
SAUCE

dash TABASCO SAUCE

SALT AND PEPPER TO TASTE

ICE CUBES

GARNISH

LEMON WHEEL

CELERY

Method

Blend all ingredients together,
then serve in glass with extra
ice, garnished with celery stalk,
mint sprig and slice of lemon.

Vodka Collins

Ingredients

GLASS

10 oz/285mL HI-BALL GLASS

MIXERS

1 oz/30mL VODKA

CRACKED ICE

1 teaspoon SUGAR

1 slice LEMON

JUICE 1 LIME

SODA WATER

GARNISH

1 MARASCHINO CHERRY

LEMON WHEEL

Method

Shake all ingredients and strain into glass. Top up with soda water. Garnish with lemon wheel and cherry and serve with straws.

Vodkatini

Ingredients

GLASS

3 oz/90mL COCKTAIL GLASS

MIXERS

1 oz/30mL VODKA

CRACKED ICE

1 dash DRY SHERRY

GARNISH

1 LEMON RIND

Method

Stir all ingredients in mixing
glass and strain into glass.
Garnish with lemon rind
and serve.

Waldorf

Ingredients

GLASS
4 oz/125mL COCKTAIL GLASS

MIXERS
1 oz/30mL BOURBON

1 teaspoon PERNOD

1 teaspoon SWEET VERMOUTH
(ROSSO)

2 dashes
ANGOSTURA BITTERS

ICE CUBES

GARNISH
ORANGE TWIST

Method

Shake all ingredients over ice
and strain into glass. Serve
garnished with an orange twist.

Comments: Reputed to be
a cocktail from America's
'Prohibition Era' in the 1920s.
The name Waldorf Astoria
is one of New York's most
prestigious hotels.

Wallington Special

Ingredients

GLASS

10 oz/285mL FOOTED HI-BALL GLASS

MIXERS

6 STRAWBERRIES

1 oz/30mL STRAWBERRY LIQUEUR

7 oz/200mL PINEAPPLE JUICE

1 oz/30mL VODKA

½ EGG WHITE

½ oz/15mL SUGAR SYRUP

CRACKED ICE

GARNISH

1 STRAWBERRY

Method

Blend all ingredients with ice and pour into glass. Garnish with small strawberry on side of glass and straw.

Comments: Delicious fruity blend.

Ward

Ingredients

GLASS

3 oz/90mL COCKTAIL GLASS

MIXERS

1½ oz/45mL CANADIAN CLUB
RYE WHISKEY

½ oz/15mL POWDERED SUGAR

1 oz/30mL LEMON JUICE

CRACKED ICE

⅓ oz/10mL GRENADINE CORDIAL

GARNISH

LIME SLICE

Method

Shake all ingredients with ice
and strain into glass. Serve
garnished with lime slice.

Water-Bubba

Ingredients

GLASS

1½ oz/45mL CORDIAL EMBASSY

MIXERS

½ oz/15mL CHERRY ADVOCAAT

½ oz/15mL ADVOCAAT

½ oz/15mL BLUE CURACAO

Method

Pour Advocaat into Cherry Advocaat, then layer the Blue Curacao. Shoot.

Comments: The advocaat resembles an egg yolk, with veins of Cherry Advocaat. Also known as an Unborn Baby.

West Indies Yellowbird

Ingredients

GLASS

7 oz/200mL FOOTED HI-BALL GLASS

MIXERS

1 oz/30mL DARK RUM

½ oz/15mL BANANA LIQUEUR

½ oz/15mL GALLIANO LIQUEUR

1½ oz/45mL PINEAPPLE JUICE

1½ oz/45mL ORANGE JUICE

CRACKED ICE

GARNISH

PINEAPPLE WEDGE

CHERRY

TWIST ORANGE RIND

Method

Blend all ingredients with ice and pour into glass. Garnish with pineapple wedge, cherry and orange twist.

Whisky Sour

Ingredients

GLASS

5 oz/145mL WINE GLASS

MIXERS

1½ oz/45mL GRANT'S SCOTCH WHISKY

1 oz/30mL LEMON JUICE

½ oz/15mL SUGAR SYRUP

½ EGG WHITE

CRACKED ICE

GARNISH

1 RED CHERRY

1 LEMON SLICE

Method

Shake all ingredients with ice and strain into glass. Garnish with red cherry at bottom of glass and slice of lemon on side.

Comment: A great appetizer before dinner. Shake vigorously so the egg white gives rise to a frothy head after straining. Some people prefer a 5 oz/ 145mL cocktail glass.

Whisper

Ingredients

GLASS

10 oz/285mL POCO GRANDE GLASS

MIXERS

1 oz/30mL STRAWBERRY LIQUEUR

1 oz/30mL MANGO LIQUEUR

1 oz/30mL LIME JUICE

1 oz/30mL LEMON JUICE

1 PEACH

ICE CUBES

GARNISH

1 STRAWBERRY

ORANGE WEDGES

Method

Blend all ingredients with ice and pour into glass. Serve garnished with strawberry and orange wedges.

White Lady

Ingredients

GLASS

5 oz/145mL COCKTAIL GLASS

MIXERS

1 oz/30mL GIN

$^1/_2$ oz/15mL LEMON JUICE

$^1/_2$ oz/15mL SUGAR SYRUP

$^1/_2$ EGG WHITE

ICE CUBES

GARNISH

twist LEMON RIND

Method

Shake all ingredients with ice and strain into glass. Garnish with a twist of lemon.

White Magic

Ingredients

GLASS

CORDIAL (LEXINGTON) GLASS

MIXERS

BITTER ALMONDS
⅔ oz/20mL CHERRY BRANDY
⅔ oz/20mL VANILLA ICE CREAM

Method

Pour cherry brandy onto
bitter almonds in glass then
float ice cream.

Widow's Kiss

Ingredients

GLASS

3 oz/90mL FANCY COCKTAIL
GLASS OR BEER GLASS

MIXERS

1 oz/30mL CALVADOS APPLE
BRANDY

$^1/_3$ oz/10mL BENEDICTINE

$^1/_3$ oz/10mL YELLOW
CHARTREUSE

1 teaspoon ANGOSTURA BITTERS

CRACKED ICE

GARNISH

1 STRAWBERRY

Method

Shake all ingredients over ice
and strain into glass. Garnish
with a floating strawberry.

Witch's Kiss

Ingredients

GLASS

12 oz/340mL HI-BALL GLASS

MIXERS

5 oz/145mL TROPICAL FRUIT JUICE

dash LEMON JUICE

dash SUGAR SYRUP

1/2 oz/15mL GRENADINE CORDIAL

SODA WATER

ICE CUBES

GARNISH

LEMON SLICE

Method

Shake all ingredients except soda water with ice and pour into glass. Top up with soda water. Garnish with lemon slice on side of glass. Serve with straws and other decoration.

Comments: A light tropical flavor.

Woodstock

Ingredients

GLASS

5 oz/145mL OLD FASHIONED
SPIRIT GLASS, SUGAR-FROSTED
USING MAPLE SYRUP

MIXERS

1 oz/30mL GIN

$\frac{1}{3}$ oz/10mL LEMON JUICE

$\frac{1}{3}$ oz/10mL MAPLE SYRUP

2 dashes ANGOSTURA BITTERS

ICE CUBES

Method

Shake all ingredients over
ice and strain into glass, then
add more ice cubes. Garnish
with a straw.

XTC

Ingredients

GLASS

3 oz/90mL COCKTAIL GLASS

MIXERS

1 oz/30mL TIA MARIA

1 oz/30mL STRAWBERRY LIQUEUR

1 oz/30mL FRESH CREAM

CRACKED ICE

GARNISH

STRAWBERRY

WHIPPING CREAM

CHOCOLATE FLAKES

Method

Shake all ingredients with ice and strain into glass. Garnish with butterflied strawberry placed on side of glass, twirl whipped cream over strawberry and sprinkle over chocolate flakes.

Comments: X-rated, tall and cute! Enjoy the ecstasy of this cocktail before you dance all night long.

cocktails Z

Zandaria

Ingredients

GLASS

8 oz/230mL COCKTAIL GLASS

MIXERS

1 oz/30mL BRANDY

1 oz/30mL TIA MARIA

4 oz/125mL FRESH CREAM

CRACKED ICE

GARNISH

1 pinch NUTMEG

Method

Shake all ingredients with ice and strain into glass. Sprinkle with nutmeg to serve.

Zed

Ingredients

GLASS

7 oz/200mL MARGARITA GLASS

MIXERS

1 oz/30mL GIN

1 teaspoon SUGAR

1 oz/30mL MANDARIN NAPOLEON

3 oz/90mL PINEAPPLE JUICE

CRACKED ICE

GARNISH

½ LEMON SLICE

1 MINT SPRIG

Method

Shake all ingredients with ice and strain into glass. Garnish with mint sprig and lemon slice.

Zombie

Ingredients

GLASS

10 oz/285mL FANCY
HI-BALL OR COCKTAIL GLASS

MIXERS

½ oz/15mL BACARDI RUM

½ oz/15mL BACARDI GOLD
RUM

½ oz/15mL DARK RUM

½ oz/15mL APRICOT BRANDY

½ oz/15mL OVERPROOF
DARK RUM

2 oz/60mL PINEAPPLE JUICE

½ oz/15mL LIME OR LEMON
JUICE

1 teaspoon SUGAR SYRUP

CRACKED ICE

GARNISH

1 PINEAPPLE WEDGE

2 PINEAPPLE LEAVES

Method

Shake all ingredients with
ice and pour into glass.
Garnish with a pineapple
wedge and leaves, swizzle stick
and straws.

Zorba the Greek

Ingredients

GLASS

5 oz/145mL FANCY COCKTAIL
GLASS

MIXERS

60mL BACARDI RUM

30mL ORANGE JUICE

15mL OUZO

15mL GRENADINE CORDIAL

ICE CUBES

Method

Shake with ice, strain into glass
and serve.

Zulu Warrior

Ingredients

GLASS

7 oz/200mL FOOTED TUMBLER GLASS

MIXERS

1 oz/30mL MELON LIQUEUR

1 oz/30mL STRAWBERRY LIQUEUR

1 oz/30mL LEMON JUICE

4 STRAWBERRIES

2 pieces CANTALOUPE

CRACKED ICE

GARNISH

1 STRAWBERRY

1 CANTALOUPE SLICE

Method

Blend all ingredients. Pour into glass. Garnish with strawberry and cantaloupe slice.

Index

COMPLETE COCKTAILS

Index

Index

Index

COMPLETE COCKTAILS

Index